Addressing Anxiety in Young Learners

Addressing Anxiety in Young Learners

A Teacher's Guide to Recognizing Needs and Resolving Behaviors

by

Sarah Taylor Vanover, Ed.D.
Kentucky Youth Advocates
Louisville

with Kristen Mennona, LPC, BC-DMT & CEDS

Baltimore • London • Sydney

Paul H. Brookes Publishing Co.
Post Office Box 10624
Baltimore, Maryland 21285-0624
USA

www.brookespublishing.com

Copyright © 2024 by Paul H. Brookes Publishing Co., Inc.
All rights reserved.

"Paul H. Brookes Publishing Co." is a registered trademark of
Paul H. Brookes Publishing Co., Inc.

Typeset by Absolute Service, Inc., Baltimore, Maryland.
Manufactured in the United States of America by
Versa Press, Inc., East Peoria, Illinois.

The individuals described in this book are composites or real people whose situations are masked and are based on the authors' experiences. In all instances, names and identifying details have been changed to protect confidentiality.

Cover image © istockphoto/PeopleImages.
Chapter photos © istockphoto.
Author photo by Jennifer Palumbo at Baby Boo Photography.

Library of Congress Cataloging-in-Publication Data

Names: Vanover, Sarah Taylor, author. | Mennona, Kristen, author.
Title: Addressing anxiety in young learners: a teacher's guide to recognizing needs and resolving behaviors / Sarah Taylor Vanover; with Kristen Mennona.
Description: Baltimore: Paul H. Brookes Publishing Co., 2024. | Includes bibliographical references and index.
Identifiers: LCCN 2023017813 (print) | LCCN 2023017814 (ebook) | ISBN 9781681256498 (paperback) | ISBN 9781681256504 (epub) | ISBN 9781681256511 (pdf)
Subjects: LCSH: Early childhood education—Psychological aspects. | Anxiety in children. | Behavior modification. | Children with mental disabilities—Education (Early childhood) | BISAC: EDUCATION / Counseling / Crisis Management | PSYCHOLOGY / Developmental / Child
Classification: LCC LB1139.23 .V359 2024 (print) | LCC LB1139.23 (ebook)| DDC 371.94-dc23/eng/20230510
LC record available at https://lccn.loc.gov/2023017813
LC ebook record available at https://lccn.loc.gov/2023017814

British Library Cataloguing in Publication data are available from the British Library.

2027   2026   2025   2024   2023

10   9   8   7   6   5   4   3   2   1

Contents

About the Author ix
About the Contributor xi
Introduction xiii

I What Is Childhood Anxiety? 1

1 Typical Childhood Development 3
Developmental Areas 9
Cognitive Development 9
Speech and Language Development 10
Motor and Physical Development 10
Social and Emotional Development 11
Self-Help Skills 11
Abnormal Development or Delays 12
Developmental Delay Versus a Mental Health Diagnosis 13

2 Generalized Anxiety Disorder 15
Case Study: Jonathon 16
Symptoms 17
Causes 18
Triggers 19
Treatments 20
Case Study: Jada 22

3 Separation Anxiety Disorder 25
Symptoms 26
Causes 27
Triggers 28
Treatments 29
Case Study: Jose 30

4 Social Anxiety Disorder ... 33
- Case Study: Ezra ... 34
- Symptoms ... 36
- Causes ... 37
- Triggers ... 38
- Treatments ... 39
- Case Study: Nora ... 39

5 Selective Mutism ... 43
- Symptoms ... 44
- Causes ... 45
- Diagnosis ... 46
- Treatments ... 46
- Case Study: Akio ... 48

6 Obsessive-Compulsive Disorder ... 51
- Symptoms ... 52
- Causes ... 53
- Triggers ... 53
- Treatments ... 54
- Case Study: Emily ... 55

7 Childhood Phobias ... 59
- Symptoms ... 62
- Causes ... 63
- Treatments ... 64

8 Anxiety and Childhood Trauma ... 67
- What Are Traumatic Events? ... 68
- Toxic Stress ... 69
- Posttraumatic Stress Disorder ... 70
- Attachment Disorders ... 71
- Physical Effects of Trauma ... 71
- Childhood Trauma Leading to Anxiety ... 72
- Trauma Prevention ... 73

II Dealing With Childhood Anxiety and Challenging Behaviors in the Classroom ... 75

9 Classroom Assessments and Professional Evaluations ... 77
- What Are Assessments? ... 78
- Noticing Differences ... 80
- Sharing Information With Parents ... 81
- What Is a Referral? ... 81
- What Does an Evaluation Look Like? ... 82
- What Do Evaluation Results Mean? ... 83

10 Comorbidities With Anxiety ... 85
- Childhood Depression ... 86
- Autism ... 87
- Attention-Deficit/Hyperactivity Disorder ... 89
- Mood Disorders ... 91
- Dual Diagnosis ... 92

11 Partnering With Parents ... 93
- Chronic Sorrow ... 94
- Stages of Grief ... 94
- Mental Health Stigma ... 96
- Parenting Children With Special Needs ... 97
- Advocating for the Child ... 99
- Stephanie's Story ... 100

12 Classroom Interventions ... 105
- Creating Routines ... 106
- Calming Strategies ... 107
- Creating Safe Spaces ... 110
- Zones of Regulation ... 111
- Incredible 5-Point Scale ... 111
- Accommodations for Social Anxiety ... 112

13 Strategies to Avoid ... 115
- Unrealistic Expectations ... 115
- Excessive Reassurance ... 116
- Creating Unnecessary Anticipation ... 116
- Showing Frustration ... 117
- Allowing a Child to Hide From Fears ... 117
- Using Belittling Language ... 118
- Offering Medical Advice to the Family ... 118
- Lack of Collaboration With Family ... 119
- Only Being Concerned With the School Day ... 120

Conclusion: Charlie's Story ... 123

References ... 129

Index ... 131

About the Author

Sarah Taylor Vanover, Ed.D., Policy and Research Director, Kentucky Youth Advocates, Louisville

Dr. Sarah Vanover has been working in the field of early childhood education for more than 25 years and has had the opportunity to be a teacher, a director, a trainer, and a college professor for other early childhood educators. She also served as Director for the Division of Child Care in Kentucky for almost 4 years, supervising Child Care and Development Block Grant (CCDBG) funding and creating child care policy. Dr. Vanover is currently Policy and Research Director for Kentucky Youth Advocates, focusing on early childhood education policy and research on positive outcomes for young children. For the past several years, she has focused her work and research on increasing access to child care for children with special needs and improving state systems that would help stabilize the child care infrastructure nationwide.

About the Contributor

Kristen Mennona, LPC, BC-DMT & CEDS, Founder, Nurture Family Counseling, LLC, Denver, Colorado

Kristen Mennona is the founder of Nurture Family Counseling, LLC, in Denver, Colorado. Her practice specializes in the treatment of pediatric eating disorders, obsessive-compulsive disorder (OCD), and anxiety within the context of the family. She is a licensed professional counselor, a board-certified dance/movement therapist, a certified eating disorder specialist (CEDS), a registered yoga instructor (RYT 200), and a Behavior Therapy Training Institute (BTTI)–trained clinician for pediatric OCD. Ms. Mennona combines best clinical practices with ancient, embodied experiences for her clients. She believes in the inherent wisdom of the body to bring forth that which needs healing.

Ms. Mennona presents nationally on the topic of body image acceptance and the integration of expressive arts. She enjoys teaching clinicians how to incorporate nonverbal methods to help clients tolerate body sensations (e.g., anxiety). She hosts an Instagram account (@the_body_as) to inspire more people to work on body image acceptance and to pass that acceptance on to the next generation. She appeared on *The Return to Embodiment* podcast in the spring of 2023.

Introduction

JAMES'S STORY

When I was pregnant with James, he was feisty. Right from the beginning, I felt like I had a soccer player living inside of me. He moved and kicked at all hours. As soon as I started to doze off to sleep, he began to move around with agitated movements. Then, once he was born, he continued to be agitated.

By the time James was 3 weeks old, we could tell that he had colic. It wasn't a huge surprise to me because his older brother had had colic and acid reflux, but James put his older brother to shame. Although we tried to avoid treating him with medication, he screamed all day long without something to help soothe him. As we looked at possible medication to reduce the pain from his acid reflux, we tried different ways to treat him. Eventually, we found a method where we could give him a liquid antacid three times a day to allow him to drink his milk without experiencing high levels of discomfort.

Once the acid reflux was under control, we started to realize that there were other factors contributing to James's challenging moods during the day. First, James never drank from a bottle. We tried different name-brand bottles that came in different shapes. We tried to hold him different ways in order to feed him, and we tried to see if different people had more success. I had nursed my first son also, but since he was in full-time child care, we had started him on bottles about 1 week into my maternity leave. This was also very helpful because when my older son, Jack, was an infant, my husband would give Jack his 2 a.m. bottle every night so that I could get several uninterrupted hours of sleep. We had plans to handle James's infant feedings in the exact same way, but James stopped us in our tracks from the very beginning.

I was still a working mother, but when James was an infant, I worked for a nonprofit agency that specialized in pediatric therapy and inclusive child care. James and I were in the same building all day, so I diligently spaced out my break time throughout the day to breastfeed him. As you can imagine, for a child who already expressed his preferences so clearly, James was difficult to wean. I had planned on weaning him at 12 months, but it took until James was 14 months old before he would drink out of a sippy cup instead of nursing.

Because James would only allow me to feed him, I was up with him frequently each night. At first, he followed a very strict routine where he diligently ate every 3 hours, so I was typically awake at 11 p.m., 2 a.m., and 5 a.m. to feed him. This changed after he turned

7 months old. It seemed as though he cried constantly throughout the night. We knew that he had had colic since he was very young. That really peaked when he was 6 weeks old. I can vividly remember a day when he cried nonstop for about 7 hours. He was fussy all day long, but at around 4 p.m. he started crying (even when I attempted to nurse him), and he did not stop until his 11 p.m. feeding. At that point, I was so tired, and my head hurt so bad, that I must have dozed off three or four times while I attempted to feed him.

I could tell that his cries as an older infant were different. He only stopped crying when I was feeding him or holding him upright. We started going to the pediatrician frequently for ear infections. The problem was that the antibiotics did not seem to make the pain subside. There were nights when we would not sleep for even 5 minutes unless I held him upright the entire night. I can't count the number of times that he fell asleep on my shoulder and then I gently (and unsuccessfully) attempted to lay him down in the crib to go to sleep. As soon as his body was horizontal, the screaming began again. My husband would attempt to take my place and console James, but he would only stop crying when I held him.

I talked to the pediatrician again and again about the constant crying. I have had epilepsy since I was 16 years old. My biggest fear was that I was not getting enough sleep and I would have a seizure. At some point, the doctor told me that I needed to turn down the volume on the baby monitor and attempt to get some rest. I was not going to be able to care for James properly if my own health was deteriorating. By the time that James was 1 year old, the doctor recommended that James needed ear tubes to reduce the number of ear infections that he was getting. He had ear tubes put in on January 7, four days after his birthday. That night he slept for 7 hours straight for the first time.

After his ear tubes relieved his pain, James was actually a quiet and reserved child. Although my husband and I talked to him a lot, he did not speak to us a great deal. His vocabulary developed quickly, so when he wanted to talk, he knew the words that he wanted to use. I just think that he was happier playing by himself. He seemed content sitting on the floor and playing independently with his toys. He loved dress-up clothes! By the time James was 2 years old, his favorite pastime was dressing up. At school, he typically wore princess dresses. He seemed to enjoy those the most. I would pick him up from school or from his church Sunday school class and he would be dressed head to toe in a beautiful princess dress and fancy shoes.

That was also around the same time that we began to let James start watching Disney movies. We had shown him some of the classic Disney movies such as *Cinderella, The Little Mermaid,* and *Sleeping Beauty.* He became obsessed with them. As soon as he was old enough to ask for gifts, all he wanted were Disney princesses. We purchased him some of the plush Disney princesses and he constantly had them by his side. Everywhere we went, we had Rapunzel, Tiana, and Merida by our side, and he slept with all of his princesses each night.

His love for dressing up also showed up in his own wardrobe. James was around 18 months old when I first bought him a baseball cap. From that point on, he never wanted to take his hat off. He didn't have a preference for one particular hat, so at least I could wash them and trade them for new hats, but he always had to have a hat on his head. He wore them throughout the day and in bed at night. At times, his child care teachers tried to take the hat off of his head for naptime in an attempt to make him more comfortable, but the struggle to take the hat away was not worth the end result. That particular fight ended quickly, however, because James stopped napping during the day before he turned 2 years old.

James always appeared to be a happy child, particularly at home, but he also enjoyed keeping to himself. When James was 2 ½ years old, I had a job change that made it necessary for James to switch child care programs. My friend, Michelle, ran a high-quality child care program that was not far from our home, and she knew both of my boys. We decided that program was the best fit for our family. On James's first day at the new center, I told Ms. Sandy, his new teacher, that James rarely took naps and under no circumstances should she take his hat away because it was like a security blanket. Michelle reinforced the idea that James should be allowed to wear his hat wherever he went.

Although the building and the teacher were brand new to James, there was one child in the classroom whom James already knew, Hannah. Hannah was just a few months older than James, and we had been going to church with Hannah's family since before James and Hannah were born. He had seen her every week in his Sunday school class, so we hoped that would be some comfort to him in a new environment. When I picked James up from his first day of school in his new classroom, Ms. Sandy told me that he had done well that day. He only cried for a few minutes after I left, and then he began playing in the classroom with the toys. He played beside Hannah and some of the other children, but he did not play with anyone else. He did follow directions when the teacher asked the whole class to sit on the rug or wash their hands, but he did not speak to anyone that day.

James did not seem to object to going to school each day, but it took almost 3 months before James began talking to his teacher. Ms. Sandy was so excited the day that she told me James spoke to her. She said it seemed like a normal conversation, as if they had been speaking each day since he started in her classroom. As soon as he started talking to her as a normal part of the classroom routine, Ms. Sandy seemed astounded by his huge vocabulary and how smart James was, but James was still very guarded. He did not speak to new people, and there were only a few classmates whom he spoke to regularly. He spoke with Hannah the most, because at this point, he spent 6 days a week with her.

Many people who James was around frequently seemed to take it as a challenge to get James to interact with them. One gentleman at our church, SJ, always attempted to get James to talk to him or at least to wave. One morning, SJ sat down next to James in a Sunday school classroom chair that was definitely made for a toddler, and he told James that he was going to sit there until James said hello. James did not utter a word during the course of the entire morning. James did not respond to challenges or when adults patronized him. He refused to speak if someone spoke to him in a baby voice, and he never spoke to people whom he did not know. If new people walked up and said hello to him, he would hide behind me and look at the floor. I constantly found myself explaining that James was extremely shy around people he did not know. Some people, especially parents of young children, seemed to understand my statement; however, others would offer me a lecture on teaching manners to my young child. What they did not understand was that I could not make him speak, especially if he was anxious about being around someone new.

During the year that James was in Ms. Sandy's classroom, he began to clearly express what he enjoyed and what he did not enjoy. James played with the pretend play toys every day, and he loved puzzles. He mostly played by himself, but he did enjoy playing with Hannah and another boy in the classroom. He chose to play with the quieter students instead of the children who incited a great deal of noise and excitement. If an adult asked James to do something he did not want to do, he specifically told them, "I don't want to do it." It became his trademark phase. When the children in the classroom hosted their annual Kentucky Derby race, the teacher asked each child in the classroom what they wanted to name their horses. James's horse was named "I don't want to do it." When the teachers interviewed the children about their mothers to create Mother's Day gifts, every answer on James's interview was "I don't want to do it."

By the time James was 3, I was looking for ways to help him be more social and interact with new children. I decided to enroll him in back-to-back 2-week sessions of swim lessons at the summer program at a local college. I was thrilled because I found a time when both of my boys could attend together. On the first day, I took the boys to the pool and Jack went happily with his group and his new instructor. James was less than thrilled about his classes, but I really wanted him to learn how to swim for safety reasons. I knew that he would be nervous the first day because he did not know the instructor, but I thought if I sat with him the first day and let him watch, then he might be willing to participate the next day.

When the children in his class were called, I stood in line with him because he looked like he might attempt to run away. The group walked to the shallow end of the pool, and the instructor had all the children sit on the side of the pool with their feet dangling in the water. I walked along and held James's hand, but when we approached the spot for the children to sit down, I could feel James pulling away. I held him firmly, and we sat down on the bottom row of bleachers about 12 inches behind the other students. I told the instructor that James might only be willing to watch on the first day, but please keep asking him to participate. The instructor was a college student, and he looked a little nervous to have an unwilling child accompanied by a parent sitting beside the water. Each time the instructor asked if James wanted to kick his feet or blow bubbles in the water, James responded by saying, "I don't want to do it!" The young man teaching the class seemed very alarmed each time he heard this. James continued to pull away from me, so I thought that if I sat on the floor next to his peers (on the wet pool deck) with him in my lap, maybe he would be able to get acclimated. He continued his dedicated response.

We came for the swim lessons every day for 3 weeks. My older son learned to perfect his freestyle stroke, and James and I sat on the wet floor while he refused to participate. I was ready for the swim instructor to throw James into the water and prove to him that it would not be that bad to get wet, but the instructor told me that was not the method he chose to use. I figured out during those 3 weeks that James possessed an iron will. I thought that I could be patient and wait him out, but I was wrong. It seemed as if James had drawn a line in the sand, and there was nothing more important to him than standing his ground. I bribed him with ice cream or a trip to the store to pick out a toy. Nothing would sway him. It just seemed as though his ultimate goal was to be right and not cave in to my request. He won. I realized during those swim lessons that I would have to completely reevaluate my approach to handling him.

James did well in his early years of preschool unless a teacher attempted to make him go to sleep at naptime. The days that I received a negative report about his behavior almost always included the phrase "he would not go to sleep at naptime." James was never disruptive at naptime. If his teacher gave him some books or puzzles and asked him to stay on his mat while the other children slept, then his behavior was not a problem. The problems arose when a substitute teacher was in the classroom and became determined to get James to go to sleep. Again, once a line was drawn in the sand about how an adult believed that James should behave, then James was determined to be right. He had a will that would not be broken. I simply laughed off these simple showdowns and joked that he would never be a child influenced by peer pressure. I still believe that his peers would have a difficult time changing his mind, but I also worry about how difficult it is for me to change his mind.

Even though James had a tendency to frustrate the substitute teachers and adults who only occasionally interacted with him, his consistent caregivers told me nothing but positive information about him each day. They always told me that he was adorable and that they loved having him in class. When he had a strong relationship with a teacher, he was extremely affectionate. When James was stubborn, his teachers seemed to find it to be an endearing part of his personality. He was extremely creative and used the vocabulary of a child several years older. The teachers loved seeing him walk into school in his hat each day. They sent me pictures of him dressed up in princess dresses in the dramatic play area of the classroom. When I picked him up from the playground, he was always playing with one of the teachers. I was so grateful that, at school and at church, his temperament did not seem to make him less loveable to the adults who cared for him each day. In some ways, I think they even enjoyed watching him dig in his heels and refuse to change his mind.

Once James decides to change his mind, the result is dramatic! When James was a 3-year-old in preschool, one mother rubbed his head each morning when she came in to drop off her own son. James has a difficult time acclimating to the classroom in the morning, so he has always needed some time to himself when he first gets to school. His preschool teachers were fabulous at asking the other students to let James have time to himself when he first arrived each morning, but of course, it is a little more challenging to ask an adult to follow the classroom rules when they enter the classroom each day.

This particular mother typically arrived about 10 minutes after I dropped James off, and he still needed that time to himself each morning. The mother would purposely seek James out each morning and rub his head. This upset James each day. Not only did he really need alone time, but he did not appreciate anyone touching him unless he initiated a hug or a high-five. Because the mother was rubbing his hat on the top of his head, James reacted strongly to his hat. After more than 2 years of wearing a hat every day, James immediately stopped wearing hats. When I offered him a hat or bought him a new hat, he yelled that he did not want to wear his hat anymore, and he threw several of his hats away. In his mind, the situation was now resolved.

By the time that James went to prekindergarten (pre-K), his vocabulary was huge, and he frequently told others that Hannah was his best friend. He loved to play in the dress-up area of his classroom, but he usually played there alone or with Hannah. He would occasionally play with other children, but he did not seek out group play. He was meeting all of his developmental milestones for language, motor skills, independence skills, and preacademics such as math and literacy. He seemed to be doing well in the classroom, but there were occasional events that popped up and stood out in my mind.

James's pre-K class occasionally had special events such as pajama day or field trips. These days always seemed to be such a challenge for James. We were always one of the first families to arrive at the child care center in the morning because I had a morning commute to get to my job in the next county. There were typically only a couple of children in the classroom when James arrived, so the teacher could tell them to let James have some personal time to adjust to the classroom. Pajama day was much more complicated. When the children dressed up for an event, all the other children wanted to see their friends as soon as they arrived at school.

The first pajama day initially seemed fine. James picked out his pajamas, and he was so excited for the day. When we walked through the door of his classroom, three children ran toward him to see his pajamas, and instantly I could tell that James did not know how to react. He seemed overwhelmed by the noise in the room and by the children running toward him. Then, I watched his face change from scared to angry. He screamed and told everyone to leave him alone. He continued to yell and went to the corner of the classroom and hid. The teacher redirected all of the other children to go back to their activities, and James screamed that he wanted his normal clothes. There was no way that I could return home to get him new clothes and make it to work on time. I left him with the teacher while he screamed about wearing his pajamas. That was the last time that he dressed up for pajama day or any other event in pre-K class.

James had similar moments whenever he had people looking just at him or even if he felt that people might look at him. The preschool and elementary children occasionally sang on Sunday mornings at our church, possibly three times during the year. James would always sing with the children in the classroom and even when the children practiced in the sanctuary. When it came time for the children to sing during the church service, James would hide under the first row of pews. Sometimes, he felt brave and would walk up onto the sanctuary steps with the other children, but before the singing started, he would attempt to walk off the stage or even run away.

Each summer, our church held a weeklong Vacation Bible School camp for our own church members and children in the community. When James was 2 and 3 years old, he wanted to attend Vacation Bible School with his brother. By the time James was finally in pre-K and old enough to attend, he was much more apprehensive. I signed both of my boys up for Vacation Bible School weeks in advance, and when summer began, Jack and I told James what Vacation Bible School would be like. On the Monday morning that it started, I put both boys in the car and began driving to the church. All of the children were supposed to gather in the gymnasium each morning to start the day singing songs together, and then the different age groups would break into smaller classes. As we walked into the gym, my older son got his name tag and found his group. I helped James find his name tag, and then he started screaming that he did not want to be there. I assumed that he was just slightly nervous, so I walked him over to his group leader. The group leader had been James's Sunday school teacher when he was a toddler, so she was not new to him. The environment was new to him. The gym was full, with more than 100 children who were screaming and running around while they waited for the singing to start. James looked at his teacher and then sprinted out of the gym. I began chasing after him, but he was much faster than I was. He ran out of the gym, down the hallway, through the church office, and out into the parking lot before I could catch him. I grabbed him up into my arms and yelled at him for running into the parking lot. I carried him back into the church, and I placed him into the arms of his teacher. Each day of Vacation Bible School drop-off got a little bit easier, but there was still a great deal of apprehension even though we were in the same church building that James was in every week since he was born.

I never knew whether James was going to wake up being nervous about his surroundings or show that strong stubborn side where he grasped for control. Usually, I could tell in the morning when he woke up what type of mood he would be in for the whole day. Some days still surprised me. One afternoon, I went to pick James up from child care, and an assistant teacher asked to speak with me. She told me that James refused to follow directions and eat lunch that day. I told her that I was fine if he did not eat because we did not force the boys to eat if they were not hungry. As she continued to tell me about the day, it seemed that she and James had gotten into a battle of wills about James sitting at the lunch table. She told James that even if he did not want to eat, he still had to sit at the table. I think her intentions were initially positive, but James decided to be stubborn once again.

Instead of coming to the table, James stood completely still in the middle of the classroom, where he initially told the assistant teacher that he did not want to eat. As she continued to tell him that he had to come to the table even if he did not want to eat, James continued to stand still and refused to speak. He stood in the middle of the room for the entire lunchtime, refusing to back down. When the lead teacher came back from her lunch break, she asked why James was standing in the middle of the room. When the assistant teacher told her that James did not want to eat lunch, the lead teacher turned to James and said, "Okay, James, go lie down on your mat if you don't want to eat." James immediately skipped over to his nap mat and sat down.

As I watched my child grow up in his child care program, I could tell that I was raising a shy, stubborn little boy. Those were temperament characteristics, so I didn't think that I would be able to change those things about him. When the center director moved children from classroom to classroom, I constantly reminded her that James needed a teacher who could trick him into believing that he was in charge without patronizing him. If James had choices and felt like he could make his own decisions, he seemed to do much better at school and at home. When I gave him a direct order with no opportunity for choice, those were the times we ended up fighting and I ended up yelling. When I could give him small choices (e.g., you can clean up now or you can clean up in 5 minutes), he seemed to do much better. I always talked to his teachers about this when we had parent–teacher conferences. The more choices that James had, the more likely he was to cooperate and follow classroom rules. If the teacher got into a power struggle with James, then he would make sure that he would win. Nothing would motivate him more than being the winner.

Because we were in a high-quality preschool, they made every effort to accommodate these needs. If James refused to sit in circle time with the class, the teacher allowed him to play in another center as long as he didn't disrupt the other children. When they gave him the option of whether or not he came to sit in the group, often he would choose to join them before group time was over. However, if it was loud or the children were too excited, he would remain by himself in the classroom. I noticed very soon that this did not seem to hinder his learning. Even though he was moving around the classroom, he was still picking up the information by listening. He would come home and sing every word to classroom songs and tell me about the weekly theme, but I knew that the teachers were not forcing him to participate.

There were some classroom activities that all children had to complete. One of those activities was the practice assessment the teacher completed with each child in order to prepare for the kindergarten entrance assessment used throughout the state. The pre-K teacher sat down with each individual child in the classroom during the semester before the children entered kindergarten in the fall. James loved one-to-one time with adults, so I was not worried about him taking the assessment with an adult with whom he felt comfortable. Actually, I was worried that, despite his knowledge, he probably would not answer a single question when I took him to the school during the summer for the actual assessment because a stranger would conduct it. After James completed the assessment with his pre-K teacher, she asked if she could speak with me about the assessment.

Immediately, I asked her if James cooperated with her about the assessment. She smiled at me and told me that he did very well on the test, but she did find one thing to be very odd. The first section of the assessment was about the child's personal information including asking him his full name, address, phone number, and birthday. When his teacher asked him to tell her his full name, James responded by saying, "You already know that." When she asked him the other information about himself, he refused to answer the other questions. Eventually, the teacher moved on and began asking the questions about colors, shapes, numbers, and other academic skills. James willingly participated and answered almost every question correctly. The teacher told me that she sensed that James was not going to answer questions that he knew she had the information about already. She also sensed that he did not want attention placed on himself. Once the attention shifted back to typical school facts, he then felt comfortable again. It seemed to me that James found the questions about himself to be patronizing, so he refused to participate. Whatever his reason, he was steadfast in his refusal. The assistant teacher tried to get him to answer those same questions the following day, and once again, he refused to tell her the answers.

As the end of the school year approached, the pre-K class began preparing a special graduation ceremony for the students and their families. The children were going to say the Pledge of Allegiance, sing several songs, and then receive their individual diplomas for graduating from the pre-K class and moving on to kindergarten. I heard James singing his songs in the backseat of the car each day as we drove around town. He knew each word to every single song, but I had no idea if he would actually participate in the graduation ceremony. I asked to take that day off from work several weeks in advance to make sure that I could attend, but I got the strong feeling that I would be sitting in the front row to watch all the other children participate in the program, not my son. I attempted to act like it would not be a big deal to me if James did not participate, but these are the types of events in which all parents want to watch their children participate. These are the rite-of-passage events that parents take pictures of and remember forever. I spent a few weeks convincing myself that I would simply take pictures of my child regardless of what he did. If he hid on the side of the stage, then that was just James being himself, and I could remember that as an accurate description.

I asked the teachers if they thought James would be brave enough to participate in the graduation. They told me that they were trying to do everything possible to make James feel comfortable for the ceremony. They were going to make sure that he was seated next to his friend, Hannah, on the stage, and they were going to place him toward the back of the stage so that he wouldn't feel as though everyone was staring at him. James was easily the smallest child in the class. Even though he had turned 5 in January, many of his younger peers were taller than he. Seating him in the back would make it impossible for me to see him, but it could make him feel comfortable enough to sing with his friends.

The day of the graduation ceremony arrived, and I was determined to be the first parent sitting in the auditorium so that I could be close enough to see James, if possible. When the class processed into the auditorium, James was actually one of the first children who walked up to the stage. He sat down in the front row and smiled at me with a huge grin. After the procession ended, he and his classmates stood up and recited the Pledge of Allegiance. James kept his eyes fixed on his teacher and never missed a word. After the pledge, the children remained standing and sang two songs about being ready to start kindergarten. James beamed down at me as he sang, and I knew he saw a huge smile plastered across my face.

When the children each received their diplomas, he proudly walked across the stage when the teacher called his name. At the end of the ceremony, I felt as if I were bouncing up and down with excitement. My shy and stubborn little boy had willingly followed directions and participated in each part of the class graduation ceremony, and I had the pictures to prove it. I felt as though this was a huge victory for our family! I knew that the summer was going to be rough for James because he would be at home with his father and brother and without a structured routine. That lack of a school routine would be a challenge, but for the moment, I was glowing over our temporary success!! What a wonderful way to end his preschool years!

When I look back at my son's first 5 years, it stands out to me how much he resisted every single change or transition in his life. As an infant, he struggled to change from nursing to eating table food. He struggled to change classrooms and to meet new children. He struggled with changes in our routine. When he was a toddler, I thought he just had a stubborn, "slow-to-warm" temperament, but as he has aged, I have been able to look at his behaviors with slightly more objectivity.

Every struggle involved a situation that he could not control. Many of his struggles involved the attention being focused on him. As an adult, fear of the unknown and fear of social attention seem like relatively normal fears, especially when we think about people who are afraid of public speaking or people whom society labels as "control freaks." I just don't think I anticipated a toddler or a preschooler to be so aware of his situations that he also had the same fears. As an adult, I worry. I worry about paying bills, doing my job well, and being an attentive parent. I don't often think about a toddler or preschooler worrying because it seems that they have little to worry about. Adults feed, shelter, clothe, and clean young children. All the basics are maintained by other individuals. Of course, there are children who DO have to worry about these necessities, but my son seemed to have all of his basic needs met. I was simply seeing misbehavior, but honestly, there seemed to be a connecting source to the misbehavior.

James had strong tendencies to strike out in anger when others paid attention to him, especially when it was the whole classroom at once (e.g., in daily circle time). He also was willing to run away to avoid the attention of others. He became very agitated when he was in an unpredictable circumstance. I didn't always identify them as unpredictable circumstances because I knew what was going to happen. The key factor was that he did not know what was going to happen because he had never been in the situation before.

It wasn't just the first time he experienced something new that he was apprehensive. It took a long time to gain his trust and for him to feel safe. There was a sense of worry that followed him much longer than other children. He relied strongly on his sense of "fight or flight" to guide him through the situations that worried him, but he also exhibited a strong defiant behavior when he completely refused to participate in a new activity or situation. I tried to diagnose him with oppositional defiant disorder or some type of behavior disorder that focused on his argumentative behavior. Eventually, a friend helped me to look at the situation and not at his behavior. That is when I noticed that the anxiety was there in every set of circumstances.

The anxiety was there when he would run away and hide. It was there when he had angry outbursts. It was even there when he would flat-out refuse to participate in a school activity (even if it looked fun to others). The anxiety took lots of different shapes. There was anxiety when others looked at him and gave him positive attention. There was anxiety there when he was experiencing a new situation or meeting a new person. There was anxiety there when I left him at school or put him into bed alone at night. He had been through no apparent trauma, but the anxiety was still there, all the time.

What I had not realized before was how much anxiety could negatively impact his behavior. I thought an anxious child would just be shy and nervous. I never imagined that an anxious child would scream and be defiant. I anticipated a child who wanted to quietly play alone, which James did occasionally do, but that was only one side of his behavior. The aggressive behaviors seemed to be taking up a huge amount of time and space in our lives, and it was a huge priority for my family to try to figure out how to help him learn to deal with his emotions in a calmer manner.

As I began to work with the counselor and occupational therapist, I learned so much that needed to be shared with James's teachers at school. I had been an early childhood special education teacher for years, and no one had ever taught me how to support a child's mental health, especially when that child was demonstrating behaviors that I did not anticipate. I began creating a "cheat sheet on how to work with James" that I gave to his classroom teachers, Sunday school teachers, and any other instructor who worked with him on a regular basis. It had instructions on it, such as:

- Social attention (even positive social attention) can be very overwhelming for James. He is uncomfortable with school dress-up days (e.g., crazy sock day, book character day) because he does not want other students and adults looking at him. He can also be very uncomfortable during birthday celebrations or "Star of the Week" activities where students are all focused on him. He has still been able to participate in these types of activities at times, but they definitely push him outside of his comfort zone.

- James frequently complains of stomachaches. We have taken him to the doctor multiple times for this discomfort. We have done ultrasounds, blood tests, and looked for illnesses such as gluten intolerance. The end verdict from the doctor is that James gets an upset stomach from anxiety. He may complain throughout the school day, but he can often be distracted and forget about his stomach when he is engaged in an activity.

- James is very uncomfortable meeting new people. Frequently, he will not speak to people until he has been around them several times. Once he knows someone, he can be a chatterbox. He has a huge vocabulary, and he can have very detailed conversations.

Many of the tips that I included on James's cheat sheet were ideas that his teachers had never thought about. Circle time is usually a teacher's favorite time of day in the preschool classroom, and most teachers don't realize that it could be the most dreaded time of day for children experiencing anxiety. Every teacher I worked with thanked me profusely. This information applied to others in the classroom. Teachers needed more training on how to work with young children who had anxiety! Because of James's story, I decided that all teachers needed more guidance on supporting the mental health needs of young children.

This book is dedicated to Michelle Falloway.
You became an honorary member of our family and helped our son through the most challenging time in his young life. No words will ever be enough to thank you.

What Is Childhood Anxiety?

Typical Childhood Development 1

To support children with different ability levels, it is important for each teacher to understand what typical development looks like in a young child. Although child development follows some essential principles, every child develops at a unique pace. Each child will develop skills in all the developmental areas, but his strengths and weaknesses will be different than another child the same age. Even siblings raised in the same home will have traits individualized to each child.

Because children develop at different rates, it can be hard for a parent to determine whether a child is just developing at his own rate or whether he is showing signs of a developmental delay. Parents should follow their instincts when it comes to concerns about their child because they are the experts. At the same time, it is important for parents and teachers to remember these key principles (Vanover, 2019):

1. *Each developmental milestone should occur within a flexible window of time.* The window surrounds the expected timeline for the skills so that children who develop a little early or a little bit later are still in the range of "normal" development. An example of this would be when a child learns to walk. The developmental milestone is 18 months, but a child who learns to walk at any time between 12 and 20 months is still considered to be on track.

2. *Although developmental milestones can occur at different points in time for each child, they typically follow a sequence.* Again, think about a child learning to walk. Children may take their first steps at different ages, but they all follow a sequence of growth. First, they crawl, and then they learn to eventually walk and run. When a child does not progress in the normal order, such as when a child walks before crawling, then there is usually something wrong with the development pattern. When a child walks first, there is typically something off about the child's gait, which the body would have naturally corrected if the child had crawled first.

3. *Typical development also occurs from head to foot (cephalocaudal) and from the middle to the other parts (proximodistal).* This principle is most easily seen in an infant. An infant can lift his head long before he has the muscle control to walk. His core muscles allow him to roll over long before the baby can use his hands and feet to effectively move. This is demonstrated in slightly older children when they are able to use muscles to make large movements before they have the refined skills to use their hands to print or use scissors.

4. *Development always moves from the simple to the complex.* This is another principle that you can easily see with motor development. First, a child learns to walk, but as a child develops, she can master more complicated movements such as running, skipping, and galloping.

5. *There are sensitive periods of time when children are best able to learn certain skills.* Language skills are an excellent example of this principle. Children are most sensitive to learning language skills between 18 months and $3\frac{1}{2}$ years old. If children are exposed to multiple languages during this time period, they are able to learn a second language much quicker than if they study it later in life. When adults attempt to learn a second language, it is a much more challenging skill because they have missed the prime window to learn.

6. *There are multiple areas, or domains, of development: cognitive development, motor development, social and emotional development, language development, and self-help/independence skills.* All five areas of development work independently and also work together throughout the body for the child to develop successfully. It can be very hard to completely isolate one area of development. For example, to look at a child's language skills, the assessor must also consider the child's cognitive ability to understand the words, the child's social ability to use words when interacting with others, and the child's motor ability to make the muscles in the mouth move in the correct patterns to articulate the sounds. All of these systems must develop and cooperate in order for a child to be successful.

7. *Children learn through play and exploring their environment.* Learning is a multisensory experience for young children. They cannot learn solely by an adult telling them

information. They must be able to hear, see, touch, taste, and feel in order to maximize their learning. Play is the best way to experience this type of learning. Play also gives children the opportunity to experiment and see how things work. A child can watch someone build a block tower, but it does not give a child information on how stable the structure is or how tall the tower can be before it falls down. Building the tower herself helps the child to receive the full sensory experience as well as the opportunity to test out a theory and prove what will work (e.g., five blocks is as high as my tower can be before it will fall down). This establishes higher levels of learning, as in the scientific method.

8. *Children develop best when their basic needs are met.* Children are designed to continually take in new information and learn, but it is hard for children to learn when their basic needs interfere with that desire to learn. If a child is not getting regular meals or enough sleep, then those basic desires will interfere with all learning systems. A child cannot think about playing with friends when his need to eat distracts from his normal interests. The same is true with his basic emotional needs. If a child is constantly worried about being safe, due to an unstable environment at home, then she will focus on her safety instead of her learning environment. The same may be true if the child is worried about the safety of a parent or the entire family.

9. *Child development is affected by a child's genetic composition and by the environment in which the child is growing and learning each day.* A genetic illness or disability can limit a child's overall development, but a rich learning environment can help that child to advance as much as possible. If a child is completely healthy, but she is limited from interacting from others and being a part of a stimulating learning environment, then that could prevent her from being at the same developmental level as her peers. For a child to be as successful as possible, she will need access to a loving and interactive learning environment, as well as proper medical treatment based on her genetic medical diagnosis.

10. *Adverse experiences during early childhood (e.g., poverty, abuse, living in a home with a primary caregiver experiencing mental illness) can have a profound effect on a child's development.* The first 5 years of development align with the largest amount of brain development. These early experiences impact a child for the rest of his life. If a child is raised in a stressful environment throughout his most vulnerable learning years, it can have a significant impact on his overall growth and development in all developmental domains.

When teachers and parents watch young children grow and develop, it is essential to be aware of what typical developmental milestones look like in order to see if the children are achieving these goals. It is also important to keep in mind the key principals, such as a developmental window for each developmental milestone instead of a child achieving these skills at exactly 2 years of age. Here is a list of the key experiences that children should meet as they progress through normal developmental milestones:

A 2-year-old child

- Can turn one page at a time when looking at a book
- Can build a tower with six or seven blocks
- Can kick a ball without falling over

- Can pick up objects while standing, without falling over
- Can run more smoothly, with a slightly wider gate than older children
- May begin toilet training
- May be able to put on simple clothes without help
- Can communicate basic needs, such as being hungry or thirsty
- Can use two- or three-word sentences
- Can understand two-step commands, such as "Pick up your doll and bring it to me"
- Has a vocabulary of about 50–300 words

A 3-year-old child

- Can be toilet-trained during daytime hours
- Can briefly balance or hop on one foot
- Can walk up stairs independently with alternating feet
- Can build a block tower with more than nine blocks
- Can copy a circle
- Can pedal a tricycle
- Has a vocabulary of several hundred words
- Can use three-word sentences
- Can count three objects
- Can use plurals and pronouns (he/she/they)
- Can ask frequent questions
- Can get dressed independently except for buttons and tying shoelaces
- Has a longer attention span
- Can act out elaborate pretend play stories
- May be afraid of monsters or other imaginary characters
- Can remember his own name and age
- Can begin to share toys with friends
- Can participate in group play, such as building a Lego tower with a friend

A 4-year-old child

- Can hop on one foot without losing balance
- Can throw a ball overhand

- Can cut out a simple picture with scissors
- Has a vocabulary of more than 1,000 words
- Can use four- or five-word sentences
- Can use past tense
- Can count to 4
- Asks lots of questions and can be extremely curious
- Can sing simple songs and repeat rhymes
- Can have a pretend friend
- Can begin to understand time
- Can compare and contrast two items
- Can be defiant when overwhelmed by rules or expectations

A 5-year-old child

- Can skip, jump, and hop with good balance
- Can walk heel-to-toe
- Can stay balanced while standing on one foot, even with eyes closed
- Can use simple tools and writing utensils
- Can copy a triangle
- Can use a knife to spread soft foods
- Has a vocabulary of more than 2,000 words
- Can use five or more words in a sentence
- Can count to 10
- Knows his telephone number and home address
- Can ask and answer open-ended questions (e.g., *how* and *why*)
- Can say "I'm sorry" when she makes a mistake
- Has a group of friends
- Likes to imagine and use pretend play
- May tell elaborate pretend stories and try to convince others they are true

An elementary school–age child (6–8 years old)

- Can show more independence from parents
- Can pay more attention to friendships and group work

- Shows a great deal of growth with cognitive skills
- Begins learning how to talk about her own feelings
- Becomes less egocentric and begins showing concerns about others
- Becomes more concerned about the opinions of peers
- Can dress and groom herself completely
- Can jump, skip, and chase easily
- Can jump rope
- Can ride a bike
- Can use tools such as a hammer or screwdriver
- Can practice skills on her own in order to become better
- Knows right and left hands
- Can tell time
- Can read age-appropriate books
- Follows three-step directions
- Can count backward
- Can name the months and days of the week in order

An elementary school–age child (9–11 years old)
- Can read well
- Can use a phone or text
- Can write letters
- Has an increased attention span
- Can see more than one point of view
- Can complete independent academic projects independently
- Becomes more independent from parents and caregivers
- Can judge in absolutes, right or wrong with little in between
- Shows an increase in large motor development, balance, and strength
- Can be very active, with a large amount of energy
- Begins to show romantic interest in others
- Finds friends very important and may have a best friend
- Becomes aware of peer pressure
- Becomes more aware of body changes as puberty approaches

- Sees adults as authority and tries to show respect to authority figures
- Prefers group work to individual projects
- Can be loyal to a group or team
- Accepts parents' beliefs still
- Admires and imitates older youth
- Develops problem-solving skills
- Approaches a mindset where she will eventually question authority

DEVELOPMENTAL AREAS

The human body is created to work as a whole; however, certain skills are more intertwined and rely on one another. Similar skills, controlled by collaborative systems in the body, are grouped together in the same domains. The predominant developmental domains include cognitive development, speech and language development, motor and physical development, social and emotional development, and self-help skills. Tracking the child's skills in each of these domains allows the parents and teachers to track the child's strengths as well as areas that need the most growth.

Although all domains have specific milestones, it can be apparent that a child is developing more quickly in one domain due to individualized strengths. Uneven development may occasionally occur even in children developing at the typical rate, simply because some stages in life focus more on growth in one domain. For example, if you look at the growth patterns of an infant, there are many different physical and motor development milestones that occur during the first year: lifting her own head, rolling over, sitting up, crawling, standing, and walking. During those large bursts of development in one developmental area, the other developmental areas may take a back seat; however, they will each have their own opportunity for more concentrated growth. Looking at the infant again, although motor and physical development are very visible during the first year, the other developmental domains are still making progress. An infant learns to smile and begins to make cooing noises. The child learns to play Peekaboo and begins to interact with cause-and-effect toys, such as a rattle. The baby also becomes deeply attached to his primary caregivers and learns to have strong relationships. All of these changes are occurring at the same time, and they affect one another.

When a baby begins to coo, it is the first step for her to learn how to use language. However, those initial coos may also be her first attempt at a social conversation when she takes turns cooing back and forth with her mother. When an infant begins to shake his rattle and realizes that it makes a noise each time he shakes it, he is also showing that he has the muscle development to hold small objects with his hand and move his muscles back and forth. Individual domains have their own separate purposes, but they constantly work together in order to help the child develop as a whole.

COGNITIVE DEVELOPMENT

The main purpose of the cognitive domain is thinking and problem solving. This domain collects information from the world around the child and processes it into patterns and reasoning. Cognitive development includes a child's creativity and her ability to reflect back on things she has done in the past, examine taking a risk, create future plans, predict what could happen in the future, process incoming information, and question current information. Cognitive development also allows a child to look at someone else's perspective and try to see another side of a situation.

For young children, the cognitive domain is what allows a child to utilize the scientific method when a child asks a question, creates a hypothesis, experiments based on the question, documents the results of the experiment, and analyzes the results of the experiment. Although many individuals learn the steps of the scientific method in middle school and associate it with a science lab setting, preschool and elementary school teachers encourage this type of learning every day. If a child is trying to determine why her block tower continues to fall down, the teacher may encourage her to make a guess at why it is falling and then test out that theory. The steps of this theory occur as the brain and the cognitive domain develop.

SPEECH AND LANGUAGE DEVELOPMENT

The speech and language domain has two primary purposes. The first is to create sounds that form words and allow the child to communicate with others. The second purpose is to help the child to understand the language that other children and adults are using and process that information to form a response to this communication, which is known as reciprocal speech. This development of speech includes how clearly a child articulates language, as well as the vocabulary and grammar that the child uses to speak.

Speech and language skills include some inferred skills, such as the tone of voice used when speaking to another, as well as the volume and intonation. It is important for children to understand that it is inappropriate to scream every conversation so that others do not become alarmed by a simple message. Speech can also include when it is appropriate to make a joke or to use sarcasm, as well as learning about situations when it is essential to use a serious demeanor.

MOTOR AND PHYSICAL DEVELOPMENT

The purpose of the physical development domain is to allow the child to grow and develop using proper nutrition and sleep. It also important for the body's immune system to develop to prevent disease and illness. The motor development portion of this domain focuses on bone and muscle development to help the child develop balance, coordination, and strength. A child who is developing healthy motor skills will be able to move about freely in indoor and outdoor environments. She can alternate her left and right legs for walking, skipping, jumping, running, and climbing.

The child will develop left-handed or right-handed preferences and develop fine motor skills that allow her to use crayons, pencils, or other tools effectively. This means that the child started off by grasping objects with the palm of her hand, progressed to pinching items between her thumb and index finger, and eventually developed the three-fingered grasp that older children and adults use to write. To effectively use writing tools, she will develop eye–hand coordination where she has the depth perception to look at an object and grab it. She will also have a strong upper body so that her shoulders and arms can effectively support her wrists and hands as she works.

SOCIAL AND EMOTIONAL DEVELOPMENT

The emotional development portion of this domain focuses on children learning about their own emotional development. Children will learn how to identify and express their own emotions. They also learn how to recognize their own needs and speak up on their own behalf. Emotional development also allows children to express their own opinions and question the opinions of others.

Development of the emotional domain allows children to reflect on their strengths and weaknesses. This helps children develop self-concept and self-awareness, which eventually leads to self-confidence once a child or a youth begins to feel comfortable with him- or herself. Once self-confidence is in place, even at a simple stage, a child begins to develop autonomy and a sense of independence.

Emotional development also allows a child to develop strong relationships with others and create a strong attachment with primary caregivers and peers. Once a child knows how to initiate relationships, she begins learning how to maintain and sustain those relationships over a longer period of time.

The social portion of the domain focuses on helping children develop healthy interactions with others and learn how to follow social expectations of society. Whereas the emotional portion of the domain helps children to become aware of themselves, the social portion of the domain helps children to develop awareness of others. Social development begins when young children play beside each other (parallel play) and then begin to play collaboratively and cooperatively together. Parallel play does not include children initiating peer interaction, but as the children become more comfortable playing beside one another, they then progress to feeling comfortable talking to one another and eventually asking another child to participate in their play.

Once children feel confident playing together, they are then in a place to begin creating friendships. They become interested in each other and start conversations about common interests. They feel safe enough to share their opinions and private thoughts. They also learn how to accept diversity and show empathy for others. The initial attached relationships that a child develops as an infant are essential in order to develop these higher level friendships as children and youth. Children must start by sharing space, toys, and even caregivers, and eventually they are able to show respect for their peers and the adults they interact with each day.

SELF-HELP SKILLS

The purpose of the self-help domain is for children to learn how to be autonomous and successfully complete tasks that they will need for daily living. These types of skills include hygiene, dressing, feeding, toileting, chores, and other skills that allow the child to be independent. These skills may also be called daily living skills.

In order to develop these skills, other developmental skills must be in place including hand and finger strength, hand control, object manipulation, expressive and receptive language, planning, compliance, and sensory processing. Self-help skills are some of the first skills that require planning skills for children, such as thinking through the process of getting dressed or feeding oneself. These skills build on foundational skills from other domains, but their overall purpose is to create autonomy and independence for the child.

ABNORMAL DEVELOPMENT OR DELAYS

Abnormal development, or a developmental delay, means that a child is not achieving his developmental milestones within the expected time period. This could be isolated to one developmental domain, or the child could show delays across multiple domains. A delay could be minor and resolve in a short time, or it could be significant and require the family to speak with a specialist to obtain additional support.

A delay does not necessarily mean that a child has a disability or a medical condition. For example, a child who has not started to walk by 20 months of age may not have a disability such as cerebral palsy. Instead, the child may need some additional support from a physical therapist to improve muscle development, and the family may need to make a purposeful effort to make the child walk instead of carrying him when he asks. For some children, those modifications to the environment may be enough to help the child catch up with the typical developmental milestones. In other cases, the delays may be significant enough that a diagnosed disability and long-term treatment may be involved. A teacher will not be able to make this kind of determination. A teacher may document what he observes in the classroom to provide the family with additional information, but the child's pediatrician should be contacted for further medical assistance.

Developmental delays can be temporary when a child gets extra assistance at a young age. This assistance is often called *early intervention,* and it means that the child may be receiving speech therapy, occupational therapy, physical therapy, or another type of specialized treatment to help the child reach typical developmental milestones. Many children who receive early intervention will never be diagnosed with a disability. They only needed that additional support for a short time during their early development.

There is not one specific reason for a developmental delay. The most common reasons include genetic reasons, complications at birth, or environmental factors. Genetic reasons for developmental delays often include the child having a medical condition passed down through the family. This type of developmental delay is more likely to be associated with a disability; however, it is not necessarily due to a disability. Birth complications, especially due to premature birth, can be another reason for a developmental delay. In this case, the child did not fully develop in utero or there was a complication during the birthing process that may take the baby some time to overcome. The developmental delay may not be permanent, and the earlier the therapy starts, the better the expected outcomes may be for the child. The final factor is the child's environment. If the child is born into a high-stress environment, then a perfectly healthy child can have a difficult time meeting typical developmental milestones. Also, the level of interaction in the environment can have a large impact on an infant or young child. The more the caregivers talk to, read with, and play with the child, the more likely the child will meet or exceed her developmental markers. If caregivers limit their interaction with the child, then she may struggle to meet these milestones.

DEVELOPMENTAL DELAY VERSUS A MENTAL HEALTH DIAGNOSIS

A developmental delay can be significantly different from a mental health diagnosis, so it is important for parents and teachers to keep this in mind. It is possible for a young child to show a developmental delay in the area of social and emotional development. This may be visible from watching the child interact with other children his age, or the teacher may use a classroom tool created to show the parents which social and emotional skills the child has mastered compared to the skills he is still working on mastering. That type of information simply shows the child's strengths and weaknesses. The teacher can use that information when creating lesson plans for the classroom setting, and the parent can share that information with the pediatrician if he or she wants to express overall developmental concerns.

When a medical professional is worried about the potential of a mental health illness, the doctor will refer the parent to a specialist who can evaluate the child for a specific diagnosis. This may be a licensed counselor, a child psychologist, or a child psychiatrist. The specialist who is contacted will advise the family on the diagnosis and the plan of treatment. A diagnosis is not an education classification, but it is a much more permanent condition, so the family will need to seek support outside of the education system to ensure that the child gets the proper support. A teacher may be the first person to notice symptoms of the illness; however, the teacher will not be the primary point of contact to make sure that the child receives the appropriate treatment.

Generalized Anxiety Disorder 2

Although there are several different types of anxiety, generalized anxiety disorder (GAD) is by far the most pervasive (NASP, 2022). Children who are diagnosed with GAD have very high levels of anxiety across a wide range of situations with no obvious triggers for their attacks (NASP, 2022). The level of the child's worry may not match the severity of the situation. The child may have the same level of anxiety over the death of a loved one as she does for a substitute teacher. These children often have perfectionist tendencies and have a hard time dealing with less than perfect behavior.

Children with GAD worry almost every day (Nemours Children's Health, 2022a). They have some of the same worries as other children their age, such as fear of the dark or monsters in the closet, but they also worry about much more serious issues like war, natural disasters, the safety of loved ones, illness, and their own personal safety (Nemours Children's Health, 2022a). This consuming worry often makes it difficult for children with GAD to focus during the day, especially on schoolwork. They also struggle to fall asleep at night when they are distracted by worrying. The same children may miss school frequently because the all-consuming worrying makes them feel sick and tired from fear (Nemours Children's Health, 2022a).

Because children with GAD worry more often and more intensely than other children, their worries can prevent them from participating in normal daily activities (Boston Children's Hospital, 2022a). Children with GAD may be misdiagnosed with conditions like attention-deficit/hyperactivity disorder because they cannot focus. Many children with GAD focus on their inability to be perfect. They are extremely self-critical, and they even begin to avoid activities where they cannot be perfect. Because of these insecurities, children with GAD frequently seek reassurance from parents, teachers, and other important adults in their lives. Even frequent reassurance only supports the children for a small amount of time, and these children fall back into a pattern of prolonged worry.

GAD can begin gradually, but without early intervention from trained professionals, it can escalate to chronic and intense adolescent and adult anxiety (Boston Children's Hospital, 2022a). This diagnosis affects approximately 3% of children and adolescents between 3 and 17 years of age, but most of those cases are diagnosed in the older age range. Although boys and girls can both be diagnosed with GAD, twice as many girls are typically diagnosed with this condition in comparison to boys.

Case Study: Jonathon

Jonathon is 6 years old and has recently been diagnosed with GAD. He continuously worries about his mother's safety when they are apart, and he worries about whether his dog is safe when they leave him at home alone during the day. His parents have enrolled him in gymnastics classes, swim lessons, and soccer, but he demanded to quit each activity when he realized that he could not immediately perform the skills perfectly. Although he has never seen a house fire, he is constantly worried that his house will catch on fire when the family is away during the day or on a vacation.

Jonathon wakes up each day and tells his mother that he has a stomachache. She has taken him to the doctor many times, but the pediatrician has found nothing that is medically wrong, such as Crohn's disease or an ulcer. After blood tests and an ultrasound, the doctor believes that the stomachaches must be related to stress. Jonathon's mother is perplexed by her son's stress level because he has not really been exposed to high amounts of stress in his life. Jonathon's biological parents are married and the family lives in the same home that Jonathon has lived in his entire life. The family has never had intense stressors like worrying where the next meal will come from or where they will live. Despite the security that Jonathon has experienced in his life, he continues to worry about situations that are unlikely to happen.

Jonathon's intense worry has led to emotional outbursts at home and at school. Sometimes, Jonathon will react by crying and screaming, but other times he will run away in the house and hide for an extended period of time. The classroom teacher has disciplined him for hiding in the classroom and not following directions, but Jonathon still refuses to participate in classroom activities when he becomes this upset. The most confusing part of this behavior is that the teacher can never figure out what triggered his emotional outburst. The teacher has asked Jonathon's mother to meet with her and make a plan for how to handle these emotional outbursts, but neither one has any ideas about how to stop the behavior from happening when they don't know what is causing it in the first place.

SYMPTOMS

When making a diagnosis of GAD, a mental health specialist will look for specific symptoms. One of the first criteria that children with GAD will display is exhibiting anxiety more often than they do not exhibit anxiety (ZERO TO THREE, 2016). It is a constant theme in the life of the child that does not go away. He or she may worry about things in the future, but the child could also be worrying about events that happened in the past. The anxiety will be based on more than one area or setting so that it is not limited to just social anxiety or anxiety about being separated from a loved one.

Other criteria for a GAD diagnosis are that the child cannot regulate his or her emotions about the anxiety (ZERO TO THREE, 2016). He may have to ask his parents for continual assurance that everything is okay. She may want her friend to constantly remind her that she likes her. There is no way for the child to avoid a sense of dread, so family members and friends must help the child work through these emotions. This can also mean that he may have aggressive behaviors or meltdowns when he feels overwhelmed by a sense of anxiety.

To be diagnosed as GAD, the anxiety must occur in different settings and in two or more relationships. If a child is only displaying anxiety at school, then that is a specific type of anxiety. For example, she may be experiencing separation anxiety due to being separated from a parent while at school; however, once she is reunited with her parents, the anxiety is no longer present.

In GAD, the child can show agitation, irritability, muscle tension, difficulty relaxing, fatigue, sporadic lack of attention, and dysregulated sleep all due to higher levels of anxiety (ZERO TO THREE, 2016). Many adults may expect children with anxiety to show only nervous or shy behaviors; however, anxiety can cause many different emotions to surface.

Many children and adults lose sleep when they are anxious because they stay awake worrying when it is time to sleep. Anxiety can also cause a great deal of fatigue for the body because it has worked so hard being anxious. In those cases, a child with anxiety may sleep for a large portion of the day to deal with the stress. A lack of focus is also a common characteristic of anxiety. A child consumed by worry may seem to be staring off into space when it is time to do schoolwork or be part of a classroom project. The symptoms of a child distracted by anxiety may appear to be like symptoms of attention-deficit/hyperactivity disorder. A skilled medical professional will be able to look at the root cause of the distraction and determine the true reason for the inattention.

Medical professionals must also make sure that the anxiety symptoms are not related to medication that a child is taking. Medications such as steroids or asthma medication may have an unintended side effect of anxiety. In those cases, a substitute medication may have the same benefits without the negative side effects. It is important to track side effects of any new medications that the child takes and to share that information with the child's doctor to see if a different medication may be needed.

There are physical symptoms associated with GAD. Many children with GAD will complain of physical pain or body aches (Bilmes & Welker, 2006). This is often stomach pain. When a child is extremely anxious, he or she will have persistent stomachaches, even to the point of developing ulcers. Unfortunately, the pediatrician must rule out all other reasons for stomach pain (e.g., Crohn's disease, celiac disease) before determining that the stomach pain is specifically related to anxiety. Headaches, heightened heart rate, persistent sweating, and pain from muscle tension may also be physical symptoms that children demonstrate.

A true case of GAD will limit the child's ability to function in his or her normal environment (ZERO TO THREE, 2016). This can be interpreted in a wide variety of outcomes. The child's anxiety may cause unnecessary hardship on the child, but it could also make it very difficult for the child to create friendships with peers and strong bonds with caregivers. The anxiety may make it challenging for a child's development to stay on track. It may prevent a child from trying new things or participating in typical classroom activities.

It is very difficult to make a diagnosis of anxiety below the age of 2 1/2 years of age (ZERO TO THREE, 2016). This is particularly true because many toddlers show separation anxiety and other fears as a part of normal development. Once a child is past these typical developmental milestones, it is easier to determine if the anxiety is a persistent problem. It is also developmentally normal for a young child to have a short bout of anxiety, such as fearing that a monster is in the closet; however, if the fears begin to last beyond 2 months and are persistent, it may be time to consider that the anxiety is more significant than initially believed.

CAUSES

Although no specific cause has been determined for GAD, there are factors that may be related to why certain individuals receive the diagnosis. The contributing factors are the following:

- Genetics
- Temperament
- Biology
- Environment

- Children exposed to significant family stressors such as family instability, poverty, or violence

Even though these characteristics may influence a child who develops GAD, children with a stable family history and a positive environment may still display a diagnosis of pervasive anxiety regardless of their family history.

Age is also a factor in GAD. Although anywhere from 9% to 20% of children may be diagnosed with some type of anxiety disorder, most of the cases are diagnosed in adolescents (ZERO TO THREE, 2016). Research has also found that higher percentages of anxiety disorders are associated with girls even though both boys and girls can be diagnosed with these types of conditions.

Anxiety is often called a comorbidity, or a condition that is frequently diagnosed at the same time as another disorder or disability. In this case, GAD is often diagnosed at the same time as conditions like attention-deficit disorder, attention-deficit/hyperactivity disorder, depression, disruptive behavior disorder, oppositional defiant disorder, and autism (ZERO TO THREE, 2016). Children with elevated anxiety frequently have a hard time processing sensory stimuli; therefore, many of these children may also struggle with a sensory processing disorder. They could be picky eaters, react strongly to loud noises, or have a hard time dealing with unique smells.

TRIGGERS

Triggers for GAD may be very different than those for other types of anxiety. Because GAD can be irrational fears and elevated worrying, the trigger may be just as irrational as the source of the anxiety. When dealing with an individual type of anxiety, the professional may be asked to look for the antecedent, the behavior, and the consequence (known as the ABC). In this case, the teacher or mental health professional would want to find out what happened right before and right after the anxiety occurred. In a case of separation anxiety, the mother may drop her child off at school for the day so the child is now left with a nonpreferred caregiver. In that case, the trigger seems logical in the progression of events.

In a case of GAD, where the child's fears may be nonstop and irrational, the progression of events may not be as logical. For example, if a child has been constantly worried about his or her home catching on fire, the trigger may be that another child in the classroom mentions his or her own home. Then, the child with anxiety may be overwhelmed with emotions due to fear of the home catching on fire, but the teacher has no visible triggers and the child is now too emotional to describe why he or she is violently crying.

In order to understand what is causing the child to become emotional or have an anxiety meltdown, it may be that the teacher and the family need to continue to document what happens before and after the anxiety outbursts in order to try and determine a pattern. This type of documentation, over days or weeks, may allow the adults to try to determine behavior patterns. For example, if a child has an outburst at the same time of day or in the same setting, adults may observe what triggers could be associated with those factors. It could also be important to look at whom the child is with when the outburst occurs, if the routines have been consistent before and after the outburst, if medication is constant or changing, and if a child's sleep patterns have changed. Big changes in a child's schedule, such as a classroom change or a parent taking a trip, may be much easier to document. Depending on the age of the child and his or her verbal skills, it may be too difficult to determine every trigger.

TREATMENTS

Depending on the severity of the child's diagnosis, the family may choose to take several different paths for treating GAD. There are therapeutic approaches and medical approaches to assist a child with GAD. There are also ways to utilize behavior therapy or occupational therapy to assist a child with regulating his or her anxiety. A family may choose one type of treatment, or they could create a treatment plan that allows them to use multiple treatments to best support the child.

Play-based therapy is the most common and developmentally appropriate method of counseling for young children. Because children in preschool and even elementary school may not be able to walk into a counselor's office and describe the source of their stress, play-based therapy allows the counselor the opportunity to interact with the child in a friendly environment. The counselor can develop a relationship with the child and interact with them in a safe environment. Then, once the two are engaged in play together, the counselor can begin to interject questions about how the child is feeling. If the child's language skills are limited, the counselor may be able to help him or her describe their fears through drawing, playing with dolls, or other nontraditional methods.

When the child's level of anxiety and reactions to triggers begins to affect every member of the family, then family counseling may be the most appropriate treatment. In family counseling, the counselor may choose to meet with the children and adults separately or to meet with the family as a whole. Again, play-based therapy may be the most appropriate when speaking to the youngest members of the family; however, the adults may need counseling on how to interact with their children during these fits of anxiety or on how to redirect the children's negative behaviors. GAD rarely affects only one member of the family, so it can help to make sure that all the caregivers have a unified approach on how to support the children as they deal with their anxiety. The adults may be overwhelmed and fatigued from supporting their children and need counseling of their own.

It is also possible that the child's support team of medical and mental health professionals recommend parent education for the primary caregivers. Parent education can look very different depending on the professional who offers the support services. Some professionals offer education in the form of a book club or a support group. Parents experiencing the same situations may meet on a regular basis to talk about their children's symptoms and how they are trying to help their children. This may include some homework, such as reading a book together outside of the group time. Other professionals offer parent education as a type of class where the child's primary caregiver comes to class, sits at a desk, and learns about the theories on how to help children experiencing anxiety.

If a parent or caregiver is attending counseling or parent education, it is also possible that he or she may need additional information or guidance from the child's teacher. Because a teacher spends up to 7 or 8 hours a day with the child while he or she is awake. It is possible for the teacher to see behaviors that a parent may not have the opportunity to observe, especially when the child is in a group setting. The whole evaluation process for a child with anxiety can include the teacher offering information for behavioral assessments, but the teacher's job does not end after the diagnosis is offered. Every time part of the child's therapy plan or treatment play is altered, the teacher is in a wonderful place to observe behavior changes that accompany the plan.

If a child experiences severe anxiety, the child's doctor may recommend medication treatment to help the child be as successful as possible. Every doctor and family is going to look at this treatment option in a different way. One of the key factors involved in choosing medication is whether the family can continue to function at the child's current level of anxiety. If the child's anxiety level is so high that it is making normal family activities very challenging, then a doctor may recommend medication as a relief for the child and for the family as a whole.

Although pediatricians can prescribe anxiety medication, many pediatricians will recommend that a young child see a child psychiatrist in order to make sure that the medication and dosage are exactly what the child needs for their condition and development (e.g., height and weight). Once the psychiatrist starts a child on a particular course of medication, it is essential to observe specific details about how the child is reacting to the medication. The doctor may not choose to place the child on a full dose initially. Instead, he or she may start the child out on a small dose and build up to the full amount of medication.

It is also critical to remember that not every child will react positively to a new medication. There may be behavioral or medical side effects to a medication; because the child is with the teacher for a large portion of the day, it may be the teacher who first sees these side effects. It is essential for the teacher and the child's parents to communicate closely during these medication changes. For example, if a child begins a new medication and sleeps during large portions of the school day, it is possible that the dose is too large and the child is overmedicated. This is essential information for the family and the medical professionals. Teachers need to make sure to share this type of observation frequently and regularly.

Many teachers have strong feelings about placing young children on medication for behavioral disabilities or mental health needs. Despite any personal feelings the teacher holds, it is not the teacher's job to discourage the family from any specific type of intervention that the child may need to be successful. The primary role of the teacher is to support the family once they pick a treatment plan for the child. This includes encouraging the family that they are trying to take care of the child to the best of their ability when the child has challenging days. It also includes documentation of the child's reaction to the medication, as well as communicating those observations to the family.

It is important for teachers to remember that they are there to *observe* when these medical and mental health treatments are put into place. The teacher should not diagnose that the child is taking too much medication because the teacher is not a medical professional. Instead, it is more appropriate for the teacher to observe that the child frequently falls asleep in class since she began taking her new medication and to tell the family that they might want to share that information with the child's doctor. Veteran teachers have been in the classroom for years and have seen children with a variety of diagnoses. Many teachers may be accurate in their assumptions of the child's medical condition and side effects; however, it is always better to present the information to the family in the form of an observation so that the family never comes back to the teacher with accusations about a false diagnosis.

Once a family completes their child's treatment plan with the help of a medical professional or mental health specialist, it can be beneficial to the child and the teacher for the family to schedule a parent–teacher conference in order to share the details of the plan and have all of the important people in the child's life using the same plan of action. However, it is also important for teachers to remember that a medical or mental health treatment plan is confidential medical information. The family may not want to share this information with anyone in order to keep labels and bias away from their child. No matter what the family decides, they are attempting to work in the child's best interest. The teacher can always remind the family that he or she is there to help in any way possible. Once that invitation has been extended, it is up to the family to include the teacher any further.

Case Study: Jada

Jada is a 10-year-old girl in fourth grade at an accelerated school in Colorado. She began reading at age 4 and by age 6 was reading chapter books without assistance. She is highly verbal but struggles to connect with her peers. Her parents describe her as serious and empathic. She is a deep thinker and a deep feeler. Jada approaches her schoolwork with intense perfectionism that can be debilitating at times. She often feels unsafe and panicky due to her thoughts about shootings both at school and in her community. She complains of frequent stomachaches and worries that something is seriously wrong with her body. She has needed to miss several days of school this year due to physical complaints, worries about completing assignments adequately, and fear of school shootings. Physical causes for her symptoms have been ruled out by her medical team. Her parents decide to seek counseling services to help her gain skills in managing the following:

- Intense fear regarding shootings at school and in her community
- Somatic complaints
- School perfectionism
- Social relationships

Jada was born right on her due date. She was a healthy baby girl and breastfed easily but frequently. Her mother notes, "It was like I could not quench her thirst, but I think her thirst was for physical closeness to me. She didn't eat for a long time when she was breastfed but requested it often." Just 20 minutes after eating, she would cry to be fed again. Her language developed early, and she walked on time. Jada had a big startle response; if she heard a loud noise, her body would jolt as if struck by an electric current. "It startled me too," her mother shared. When Jada was startled, it would take at least an hour before she returned to her baseline state. She had frequent stomach issues that were exceedingly difficult to diagnose or soothe. Her parents tried a variety of changes to her diet to see if they could ease her pain.

Jada's parents reported that when she was 2 years old, they took her along with them to a birthday party. Upon entering the room and seeing so many faces, she began to cry. She clung to her parents. They stayed at the party for a brief time but decided to leave early because she was red-faced and crying. As they walked out of the party and got into their car, she exhaled a large, snotty sigh and began to calm herself.

When her mother left for work each day, even though this was a familiar routine, Jada would scream and cry. It often took her more than an hour to return to a calm state with her babysitter. Everyone in the family began to dread the daily transition from parents to babysitter.

When watching a cartoon with her parents, she became frightened of one of the characters in the program. Even when her parents tried to explain that the character was not "bad" or "dangerous," she was convinced he was "a bad man." For the next 2 weeks, she cried at bedtime because "Green Man" (she named him this because he wore a green shirt) would "get me!" She was traumatized by the image of Green Man for 2 years.

Her parents reported Jada having a sense of dread when school arrived, but they found that other than her initial separation, she was not too anxious. They were relieved to see her thrive in the structure of school. As she entered grade school, they noticed that her anxiety heightened when a school project was due, but her ease with learning made it possible for her to face her fears. Her parents were pleased.

Academic rigor increased in third grade and although Jada was able to keep up with the material at school, she began to become fixated on getting her assignments "just right." Her parents noticed that she completed most of an assignment only to rewrite the entire thing because "My handwriting needs to be neater." Her parents tried as best they could to encourage her to not rewrite assignments, but Jada would end up in a puddle of tears on the floor if she could not rewrite it. Her parents assumed that it was better to let her have control over this aspect of her life because they knew their daughter often seemed overwhelmed.

Jada also needed to miss school a couple of times on the day an assignment was due because "I don't have it right yet! I can't turn it in like this!" Her parents were baffled because she would spend many hours worrying and working on her projects. In two cases, her parents agreed to let her miss the day to complete the assignment because they felt she needed the extra time to let go of the product. Missing school to complete an assignment helped Jada in the moment, but her parents soon felt the pressure from her to do this more often. Her parents also felt that her accelerated school fit her academic needs in terms of assignments but found that Jada often compared her work to other high achievers at school.

In fourth grade, Jada's history class focused on the life of Martin Luther King, Jr. Jada was inspired by Dr. King and his legacy. However, as she learned about his assassination, she was overwhelmed. She talked about it often and began to have nightmares. Jada grappled with understanding that cruelty existed in her world.

During the same year, a school shooting occurred in Highlands Ranch, Colorado. Until this shooting, Jada had assumed that school lockdown drills were for potential situations that *could* happen but not that they were actual situations that occurred in the U.S. As Jada processed that school shootings have happened before and could happen again, panic surfaced for her. She reported many somatic symptoms when going to school now: pounding heart, sweaty hands, shaking, and feeling as though she needed to run out of the building.

Her newfound fears combined with her somatic complaints and her tendency toward perfectionism. This created the perfect storm for Jada. She no longer wanted to go to her friend's house for fear of panic symptoms emerging. She often complained of physical ailments that kept her from attending school. She obsessed about making sure assignments were written as though typed. She began to attempt to control her world in ways she had not previously.

Jada shared that she wants to feel better. She presented as a motivated client, eager to please her treatment team. Her parents are educated on how to stop accommodating Jada's anxiety by allowing her to miss school. Jada was referred to a psychiatrist for a medication evaluation for the beginning steps of her treatment. It was agreed that she and her parents may elect to stop medication as she feels better.

Three months into therapy, her parents have learned that her anxiety can hold the whole family hostage if they do not set limits on it. They were surprised to see that as they had faith that Jada could manage her anxiety and go to school, she was able to do just that. Jada reported an increase in her confidence. She also reported feeling more hopeful (but still scared) about her school and community. She has begun writing her homework only once and turning it in, even though she reports, "I hate it!" Her parents remind her that "perfection" is not helpful. With her parents' support, she began to go on social outings with peers. She still reports stomachaches and headaches, but the frequency has decreased and she can manage them better.

Separation Anxiety Disorder 3

Separation anxiety is a form of anxiety where a child becomes fearful and stressed when he or she is separated from home or from a loved one. This type of anxiety is developmentally appropriate when a child is an older infant or a toddler. By the time a child is 3 or 4 years old and ready to begin preschool, he or she has normally outgrown this type of anxiety. Prolonged anxiety of this kind leads to separation anxiety disorder (SAD). (Note that in this book, SAD always refers to separation anxiety disorder and not to seasonal affective disorder.) An intense case of SAD begins to interfere with the child's normal activities such as attending and participating in school or traditions and activities with family and friends (Mayo Clinic, 2022b). The older the child is, the more unusual

SAD is. Children in preschool and elementary school are more likely to have SAD than are teenagers or adults.

Because separation anxiety is typical for very young children, the more intensified version, SAD, is often seen as a gateway anxiety disorder that may lead to children having other intense fears under different circumstances (Lewinsohn et al., 2008). SAD is often identified by constant worry and intense dread about future separations, even those as simple as a child being dropped off at preschool. The intense worry will lead to both mental and physical symptoms including lack of sleep, upset stomach, intense stress in social situations, and an inability to focus in a school setting (Lewinsohn et al., 2008). This condition is not uncommon but it is probably significantly underdiagnosed, and some children have learned to live with the mental and physical symptoms instead of receiving the appropriate treatment for their condition. When the condition is diagnosed in young children, they are usually scared of being separated from a parent or primary caregiver. This is different from how it manifests when the condition is present in teenagers or adults, who tend to be stressed when they are separated from a significant other or their children.

SYMPTOMS

SAD is diagnosed when a child's separation anxiety lasts beyond the typical developmental norms. The symptoms will display differently in every child, but SAD usually shows anxiety that is much more intense than the actual situation calls for, and an episode will last as long as 4 weeks or more (Healthychildren.org, 2022). Some of the most common symptoms include the following:

- Worries too much about the safety of other family members
- Worries too much about his or her own safety
- Worries too much about a family member getting lost
- Worries too much when apart from a family member
- Refuses to go to school
- Refuses to sleep alone
- Is scared to be left alone
- Is scared to sleep away from home
- Has nightmares about being separated from a parent or loved one
- Has frequent headaches and stomachaches
- Experiences muscle aches and tension
- Has episodes of bedwetting
- Acts clingy at home with a preferred loved one
- Has meltdowns or temper tantrums at the time of separation from a caregiver
- Experiences inability to concentrate
- Has poor performance on schoolwork

- Experiences difficulty in social settings and social interactions
- Experiences irritability (due to concentrating on fears)

When a mental health professional considers diagnosis of SAD, he or she will consider all the listed symptoms but also will look for certain criteria. The child must demonstrate excessive and recurrent separation anxiety when away from home or loved ones (ZERO TO THREE, 2016). This would also mean that the child demonstrates consistent and disproportionate worry about the consequences of a separation. Children with SAD will be extremely hesitant or refuse to attend child care, school, or other environments away from home. To show how distressed they are to leave the home, these children could cry, cling to a parent, hide, or throw a tantrum.

Other criteria that the mental health professional will look for can include the child being afraid to be left alone, the child refusing to fall asleep alone, or the child having nightmares about separation (ZERO TO THREE, 2016). The professional will also look for physical symptoms of stress to accompany the emotional symptoms. The diagnosis will also consider whether the child's anxiety prevents him from doing normal, everyday activities.

CAUSES

As with most illnesses, the cause of SAD can be genetic or environmental. A child can have certain temperaments that makes her more susceptible to SAD, or it could be that he has a genetic history of anxiety in the family so it is more natural to follow in those genetic footprints (Lewinsohn et al., 2008). Children who live in the house with a parent or caregiver who is diagnosed with an anxiety disorder are more likely to share that diagnosis because they have learned their coping skills from their adult role model.

There is a wide range of environmental factors that could cause a child to experience intense separation anxiety. One of the most common causes for a child to experience this type of anxiety is an extended parental absence (Lewinsohn et al., 2008). Military deployment and parental incarceration are two very different types of parent absences; however, the effect on the child can be very similar. If a young child does not get to interact with the parent regularly, he or she can begin to worry about the parent's safety. Technological advances have made it possible for families to see each other virtually, which is helpful, but it cannot take the place of face-to-face contact and spending time with one another.

It is also possible for shorter absences to have a negative impact on the children experiencing separation anxiety. If one parent travels a great deal for work, even with trips as short as a week at a time, it can cause a child to begin to dread the next trip. He might be content when the parent arrives home, but he will soon begin to worry about what will happen when his parent leaves again.

Children are significantly affected by the loss of a parent from separation, divorce, or death. Even though a legal separation or divorce may not seem as serious in the eyes of an adult, a child can still see it as an event taking away her mother or father. Of course, the death of a parent or anyone close to the family can cause the child to begin to worry that other members of the family may die. Other significant life events, such as the loss of a beloved pet or moving to a new school, can create the same type of stress leading to SAD.

Some causes for SAD may be based more on the parenting style in the home. A parent could attempt to reduce the stress in a child's life by avoiding all possible situations leading to stress on the child. Unfortunately, this attempt typically backfires and makes the child even more afraid to face his fears after having little experience in childhood in overcoming small obstacles (Mayo Clinic, 2022b). Another factor contributing to separation anxiety is the parent's level of affection. If the parent shows a low level of warmth toward the child, the child may begin to cling to the parent even more to secure that warmth and encouragement.

The dynamics of a parent's lifestyle may also contribute to a child's SAD. A parent or caregiver with alcoholism can be a factor in a child's anxiety level. The National Institutes of Health shows that 14% of children who have parents with alcoholism eventually develop SAD (Lewinsohn et al., 2008). There is also a strong correlation between parent conflict in the home and the number of children with SAD.

TRIGGERS

The triggers for SAD can be like the events that may have caused the stress in the beginning of its development (Mayo Clinic, 2022b). One of the largest triggers for this type of behavior can be a traumatic experience such as an adverse childhood experience (ACE). The list of these traumatic events includes physical abuse, emotional abuse, sexual abuse, physical neglect, emotional neglect, a mental illness in the home, divorce, substance abuse, parent incarceration, and domestic violence. Just one of these events can be a trigger for a child who is already prone to separation anxiety or who has experienced it in the past.

Normal family life changes, such as moving to a new school or town, can also be a trigger for an episode of separation anxiety. The birth of a sibling and moving to a new house are also possible triggers. A family member's deployment or incarceration can be a trigger, as can a change in work shifts (e.g., a parent starts working the night shift, so the child does not see her as much). A child moving to a new foster home can initiate SAD, but it may be because the primary caregivers are changing and the child may not want to be separated from a teacher or case worker.

TREATMENTS

SAD does not go away without treatment; thus, when a parent notices symptoms, it is important for the parent to reach out to the pediatrician for assistance (Mayo Clinic, 2022b). When it is left untreated, the condition can escalate to other anxiety disorders or more complicated conditions such as generalized anxiety disorder. A skilled mental health professional will need to distinguish between SAD and potential personality disorders like borderline or dependent personality conditions (Lewinsohn et al., 2008). Once an accurate diagnosis is made, the appropriate treatment plan can be created.

Depending on the age of the child when the symptoms emerge, play-based therapy or cognitive-behavioral therapy (CBT) are typical treatments for children with SAD. CBT is often categorized as "talk therapy." The overall goal of this type of therapy is to help the child reprogram his or her way of thinking—the cognition patterns. The therapist will help the child identify the source of the stress and help the child find more beneficial ways to deal with his or her stress. When the child's anxiety is so intense that it affects the entire family (e.g., the child's anxiety prevents the parents from leaving the child with a family member or a babysitter even for a few hours), then family therapy may also be recommended. Parenting classes may be another option to help the parents understand how to guide the child without making the anxiety more intense.

If the child's anxiety is so intense that it limits the child's activities and the activities of the family, then the pediatrician may recommend medication for anxiety. This is another case where communication between the teacher and the child's parents is essential. Anxiety medication such as an SSRI (selective serotonin reuptake inhibitor) is the mildest type of medication for a condition like SAD, but it can have side effects that include nausea, vomiting, headaches, drowsiness, dizziness, loss of appetite, nervousness, and agitation. Because the teacher is with the child during more of her waking hours, it is essential for the teacher to communicate to the parents all of the symptoms that are present in the classroom and to document that information so the family can share it with the medical professional. It can take some trial and error to find the best medication and the best dosage for the child, so while the family is in that process, information from the teacher can be essential.

Along with therapy and medication, the family may be given instructions for guiding the child's behavior at home. Just as it is essential to follow the therapy and medication plans put into place, it is equally important to follow the behavior treatment techniques to help shape new and positive behaviors for the child.

Even though the child is distressed, it is important to still attend essential activities like school. The parent still needs to drop his child off at school, but in order to help the child cope with the separation, it is important to develop a consistent drop-off routine in order to make things predictable and comforting for the child. One way to do that is for the parent and child to create some type of good-bye ritual. The ritual gives the child some control over how to say good-bye, and the ritual can help the child to identify the attachment between himself and his parent.

It is also important for the family to find occasional opportunities to introduce the child to new settings where she may need to temporarily separate from her parents. The family does not need to force the child into these opportunities frequently, but it is important not to avoid the opportunity when it presents itself. The parents also need to continue to introduce the child to new people and visit new places when possible.

The parents and primary caregivers also need to remain as calm and consistent as possible with the child when dealing with her anxious behaviors. Agitated behaviors can lead the child to be more anxious and clingier. If the parent seems confident and reinforces the fact that she will be back soon, that can help the child to be confident as well. The parent needs to remember not to make promises that she cannot keep in order to calm the child just for the moment. A child with SAD will remember the broken promise and will be more anxious the next time. The best decision for the parent is to be honest about when he will return and to be confident when explaining that to the child. When the parent returns when he said he would, the child can develop trust.

Case Study: Jose

Jose is a 5-year-old boy with an intense fear of separating from his parents. This fear has increased in intensity over the last year, and his parents are seeking help at the request of Jose's school. His parents describe him as content unless he needs to be separated from his parents. He has no known trauma that explains his intense reaction to being separated. If he is in the near vicinity of his parents, he can easily entertain himself, but if he senses that they are getting ready to leave, he will follow them from room to room crying.

Jose's parents report trying various approaches to ease this transition for him, including talking to him about how they always return, having him practice being in the next room in the house without them, and having babysitters come over for shorter time periods. When he is separated from them, he can exhibit a variety of responses that include shutting down, crying, and throwing a tantrum. His teachers and parents agree that it appears he is trying to figure out whether he can do something to prevent the separation from happening. Once he has been separated for 30 minutes or more, he calms down but remains anxious and checks in constantly about when his parents will return.

His parents describe him as a typical baby. He used a pacifier as an infant, and his parents found that this was a useful tool to soothe him. They noted that when it was time to let go of the pacifier, Jose cried for hours each night after it was taken away. It was hard for his parents not to just give it back to him, but they held firm. Within a week of his pacifier being taken away, Jose began sucking on his fingers.

Now at age 5, he is often found with his fingers in his mouth. He uses them the same way he used his pacifier, to soothe himself when he is anxious. This usually happens when he needs to be away from his parents. Jose has an older sister, and his parents noted that when she was a baby, they were able to place her in a Pack 'N Play while they cooked dinner or did chores. When Jose was old enough to sit comfortably, they tried placing him in the same Pack 'N Play, but he would cry inconsolably unless he was held. His parents became accustomed to placing him in a child carrier and wearing it while they did their daily chores. They both report that this was exhausting, but it was not as tiring as his nonstop crying. When he was in contact with them, he happily observed their chores and liked being a part of the family activities.

At age 3, Jose was enrolled in child care because both of his parents work. It took 6 months for him to become accustomed to being dropped off at child care. Once he associated child care with being a place that Mom or Dad would leave him, he would literally dig his heels into the ground. His parents often had to carry him into the building. He would cry inconsolably with his fingers in his mouth. Sometimes, he would throw a toy or try to break something during his tantrums, but that was rare. It was clear that he was distressed and fearful. Jose felt safest with a parent by his side, but his parents needed to work to support the family. His parents were upset and often felt guilty when leaving him even though they knew his teachers were caring professionals.

His parents continue to describe their most exhausting part of the day as bedtime: Jose has made it through the school day and feels safe at home with Mom and Dad. When his parents tell him he needs to go to his own room and go to sleep alone, this does not feel safe to Jose. His mind is so imaginative, he can think of all the bad things that could happen to him at night. "What if a villain breaks in?" "What if I get thirsty?" "What if I call for help and you can't hear me? Or what if something bad happens to you?"

It seems to Jose that there are simply too many dangers to warrant being separated, and he would feel better to have everyone in the same room. Mom and Dad are tired, so they agree to do "room checks." They agree to stand between Jose's room and his sister's room and to check on them three times before bed. The first check is a kiss on the head and saying, "Good night." The second check is a simple, "I'm here until you fall asleep." The third check ideally is a parent making sure he's asleep. This process is improved from the past when Jose would fight sleep for hours for fear that his parents would leave his room. Even with this system in place, if Jose falls asleep before the third check has happened, he will jolt awake screaming, "I DIDN'T GET A THIRD CHECK!!" He is alarmed. He is frightened. His parents will start the three checks over, but this time he will make sure he knows he was checked on a third time. He's getting more sleep than he used to get, but it is still quite disruptive.

At school, once the initial separation has happened with his parents, Jose can be seen sucking on his fingers even with his face mask on. He's kind to other kids but reserved. He listens to his teachers but becomes tearful if they are not in his line of sight. He seeks out teacher support for tasks he can do on his own. He just feels better when he's in close proximity to a caring adult. Sometimes, he will have a scary thought that his parents are going to forget to pick him up and he will cry.

Social Anxiety Disorder 4

S ocial anxiety, sometimes called social phobia, is a strong fear of social settings or public performances (ZERO TO THREE, 2016). These public performances do not have to be large events, and in most cases, they are as simple as being called on in class, starting a conversation with a peer or an adult, or telling someone personal thoughts or opinions. This intense fear will cause children to avoid group settings (including school) and talking to others. Children with this diagnosis are afraid of what others may think or say about them. They believe that they will do or say something embarrassing, so rather than be embarrassed, they avoid interactions with others whenever possible.

Whether they receive positive or negative attention, children with social anxiety do not want to be the center of attention, even briefly (Nemours Children's Health, 2022a). In fact, they do not want others to notice them at all, so they desperately try to fade into the background. In a classroom, they will avoid talking to friends or refuse to participate in group activities like the classroom circle time. If the child does participate in a group activity when the teacher calls on him, he may react by freezing, panicking, or running away from the activity. An activity like a class presentation or having to stand in front of the whole class to speak can be terrifying and could bring on a reaction like a panic attack. To prevent this level of fear, the child may attempt to avoid school or friends at all costs. This reaction can potentially impact a child's school attendance or performance for many years to come.

Children with significant cases of social anxiety will also have physical symptoms (Nemours Children's Health, 2022a). Social anxiety can cause a child to experience shortness of breath, a racing heartbeat, sweating, and intense blushing. Although many children and adults may experience a mild version of these symptoms when they feel embarrassed, the child with social anxiety will have these symptoms persistently and will experience them intensely. She may also have fatigue or an upset stomach prior to a social situation when she begins to experience a feeling of dread. If the anxiety escalates to the level of a panic attack, she may become shaky, lightheaded, or even pass out.

Although generalized anxiety disorder (GAD) also has persistent and intense symptoms, social anxiety symptoms are strictly limited to social interactions and social attention. The intense fears associated with GAD focus on many different types of fears. Fear of the future would be associated with upcoming social events like attending a birthday party or a schoolwide program.

The onset of social anxiety usually occurs around the age of 13; however, young children can also be diagnosed in preschool (Mayo Clinic, 2022c). Shy children are more likely than others to experience social anxiety, but children who are extroverted can still experience this type of anxiety. The diagnosing health professional will check whether persistent social anxiety has been occurring for at least 2 months to make sure that it is not just a phase.

Case Study: Ezra

Ezra is 5 years old and has begun attending kindergarten this year. He has been in child care since he was 18 months old, so he is already accustomed to a classroom setting. He was very nervous to start a new school, especially a school so large, but the school was prepared for the kindergarten transition process. Two weeks before school started, the school offered a kindergarten breakfast for all the incoming students. All of the kindergarten teachers were there, and they offered the students tours of their classrooms. After the tour, Ezra's parents felt comfortable, and he enjoyed meeting his teacher.

During the first month of school, the teacher noticed that Ezra is rarely in a group with other students. When the class sits down on the rug together for calendar or group learning, Ezra immediately asks to go to the bathroom. After noticing this pattern, the teacher began asking Ezra to go to the bathroom before the group time started. Then, Ezra seemed to have a difficult time finishing his table work and lagged at his desk while the other students moved to the rug.

In order to get to know all of the students better, the teacher has the students take turns taking home Tommy the Frog, the classroom stuffed animal, and the students take pictures of Tommy with their family over the weekend. Most of the students can barely

wait for their turn to take Tommy home, but when it was Ezra's turn, he left Tommy at school on Friday afternoon.

The students in Ezra's class received an award for perfect attendance during the first month of school, so they earned a pajama party. The teacher made sure that every family knew that students had the opportunity to wear their pajamas for the day and even bring a stuffed animal. When Ezra arrived at school, he was wearing his normal jeans and a t-shirt. When the teacher asked him if he wanted to wear pajamas, he would not answer the question.

One of the school cafeteria workers came to the classroom to speak to Ezra's teachers because she had some concerns about his behavior in the lunch line. Each day, when the children go through the lunch line, they have a choice between two different entrees. In order to reduce the spread of illness, the cafeteria workers keep the trays out of reach of the children until the child tells them which entrée he or she wants. The cafeteria worker was concerned that Ezra will not tell the staff what he wants to eat and then the line begins to back up while they try to guess what Ezra would like that day.

The teacher has heard the students frequently talking about birthday parties in the classroom. The school policy states that in order for the school to send home birthday party invitations, a child must invite every child in the classroom. The school families have been complying with the policy, and the teacher has been distributing invitations quite frequently because several of her students have turned 6 years old. During reading group one day, several of the students were talking about Ben's birthday party from the past weekend. The teacher asks Ezra if he attended the party. Ezra did not respond, but the child sitting down at the table next to him said that Ezra never goes to birthday parties.

After thinking back on some of Ezra's behaviors in the classroom, the teacher decides it is time to have a conference with Ezra's parents to talk about how he is adjusting to the social environment in the classroom.

SYMPTOMS

When considering the symptoms of social anxiety, it is important to remember that the child is attempting to avoid the embarrassment of social attention, so all symptoms will have that as a root cause. Overall, fear is motivating many of the child's behaviors. A child with social anxiety may demonstrate some of the following behaviors, symptoms, and thoughts:

Behaviors

- Refusing to go to school
- Avoiding participating in a group activity
- Avoiding going places away from home
- Asking a parent to stay with him at activities where other children are dropped off
- Declining invitations to play dates or birthday parties
- Not answering the teacher in front of the class
- Crying or having a tantrum
- Mumbling
- Making poor eye contact
- Staying home on the weekends
- Not ordering her own food in a restaurant and deferring to the adult to order
- Not talking on the phone or texting
- Being afraid to eat in front of others
- Being afraid to use public restrooms
- Being afraid to express his opinions, wants, or needs

Physical Symptoms

- Stomachaches
- Blushing
- Sweating
- Shaking
- Muscle tension
- Irritability

Frequent Thoughts

- "I am such an idiot."
- "I will probably say something stupid if I talk to them."
- "They won't like me or want to play with me."
- "The other kids can tell I'm scared."

Although fear may be the primary cause of the child's anxiety, with social anxiety, the child may also be experiencing embarrassment, shame, sadness, anger, and helplessness. The child may fear new settings and activities because she doesn't know what type of social activities she will encounter. If she realizes that she can work or play independently, then her anxiety level may decrease once she has arrived. However, if she goes somewhere new and it ends up being an activity that requires group play and a lot of social interaction, then her anxiety level could elevate quickly.

When a medical professional looks at a child's symptoms and behaviors to diagnose social anxiety, the professional will look for several key characteristics. First, the diagnostician will check whether the fear of social interactions or social performances is persistent and not just in one setting or for a short period of time (ZERO TO THREE, 2016). He will also look to see how the child relates to unfamiliar people or to scrutiny from adults or peers. The professional will look to see whether the amount of fear the child experiences is proportionate to the type of activity in which the child is participating. If the child's fear is at an irrational level, then that brings up other concerns.

It is important for the diagnostician to see whether the child is avoiding social interactions due to the child's fear. He also looks to see what type of emotions or behaviors are brought on by the anxiety. Typically, he checks for panicking, crying, tantrums, freezing, running away, clinging to a familiar adult, or not being able to speak in front of others. When the diagnostician is making a diagnosis for social anxiety, he needs to make sure that other anxious behaviors (present in other diagnoses) are not present in the child's behavior (ZERO TO THREE, 2016). If it seems that the child has more fears than social interactions, then the diagnosis may be more complex.

Finally, the diagnostician will look to see how the fear and anxious behaviors affect the child and the family (ZERO TO THREE, 2016). For example, a child with social anxiety will be afraid to attend birthday parties, go to his family's place of worship, or even have age-appropriate friendships. The same child may be afraid to participate in school activities and start to fall behind developmentally. If the child's anxious behaviors are so intense that it prevents the entire family from going out to eat dinner in a restaurant or attend a house of worship, then the entire family's culture is being affected by the anxiety. Another child may be willing to attend group activities, but she may require that a parent stay at those activities with her to ease the anxiety. Again, in this case, the social anxiety is affecting members of the entire family and limiting the family's ability to participate in its normal routines and activities.

CAUSES

As with many health conditions, genetics, temperament, and environment can all be causes in a child developing social anxiety (Mayo Clinic, 2022c). Although it would be difficult to isolate a specific gene that determines social anxiety, there is an obvious trend that this type of anxiety runs in families, which is why medical professionals ask for a family history at the beginning of the diagnosis process. Also, some children have a temperament that makes them more vulnerable to this type of anxiety. For example, shy children are more likely to be diagnosed with social anxiety than children who are more outgoing and boisterous.

Social anxiety can often be linked to the environment in which a child grows and develops. For example, children who grow up experiencing consistent teasing, ridicule, or humiliation are going to be much more likely to develop social anxiety (Mayo Clinic, 2022c). This type of teasing can begin at a very young age, and it generally is very intense to cause a child to develop so much fear and stress in social situations. Bullying by peers or family members can also contribute to social anxiety.

Children with overbearing parents are also more likely to show signs of social anxiety (WebMD, 2022). In some ways, this type of aggressive parenting can have the same result as bullying. Children become afraid of social interactions due to the family interactions, and then they begin avoiding interactions with all others. They also become fearful that other adults will approach them with anger or criticism. One of the common symptoms of social anxiety is that children are afraid of criticism and disappointment from those around them. A home with overbearing parents may cause those types of fears to easily develop in young children.

Children who have experienced trauma and abuse have been placed in the type of environment that can easily create high levels of anxiety (WebMD, 2022). A child who experiences verbal or physical abuse will easily begin to question his intelligence, his ability, and his worth. Children with social anxiety will also begin to ask these important questions because they fear saying something or acting in a way that would create shame or embarrassment. In an abusive home, the adult may already tell the child that he or she is an embarrassment, causing the child to question himself even sooner than a child who lives in a more nurturing environment.

When a child has experienced the trauma of being abandoned by a parent or being placed in foster care, then she is much more likely to question why the parent left. Embarrassment and shame of the child are typically two of the first reasons the child thinks of, even if the child was placed in foster care because the parent was not capable of caring for the child at the time of removal. The early timing of the trauma, and the frequency of the trauma, can have an impact on the age at which the child is diagnosed with social anxiety.

Social anxiety can develop slowly over time as a child experiences more and more stress during typical social interactions (NSAC, 2022). It is also possible for a child to experience one traumatic event that causes an immediate fear of social situations from that point onward.

TRIGGERS

The root of social anxiety is fear—predominantly fear of being judged by others and by oneself. It is also a fear of not fitting into social norms. This means that triggers for social anxiety include situations where a child feels judged. Potential triggers for social anxiety include the following:

- Meeting new people
- Making small talk with others
- Being the center of attention (e.g., Student of the Week)
- Meeting someone the child believes is "important"

- Attending a school dress-up day (e.g., Crazy Hair Day, Pajama Day)
- Performing on a stage
- Being teased or criticized
- Being watched while doing something

TREATMENTS

A treatment plan for social anxiety can involve therapy, medication, and/or behavioral supports. The severity of the case will determine how many types of treatment will be used, and the medical doctor and mental health professional involved in the diagnosis process will guide the family through choosing among the recommended treatments for the best options. Because treatment is confidential, families may keep that information to themselves. It is always best for the teacher to let the family know that he or she is willing to support them as necessary, and that may be the initial gesture that helps the family share valuable information with the school.

Counseling for the child and the family (depending on how much the family is impacted) will always be an available option for the family. Because more children are older than preschool age when diagnosed with social anxiety, the first choice may be cognitive-behavioral therapy (CBT) for the child. CBT is used to treat conditions such as anxiety and depression, and the purpose is to help the child identify negative patterns of thought about himself and about the world around him. Once those patterns are identified, the therapist helps the child to face his fears instead of avoiding them. CBT also helps the child to learn how to calm his body and his mind when he begins to be stressed or fearful. The family may choose to look at family counseling to determine how the child's anxiety is having an impact on the whole family's activities and emotions.

Medication is another option for treating social anxiety. The most common type of medication used to treat social anxiety is a selective serotonin reuptake inhibitor (SSRI). This type of medication is less controversial than psychotropic medication, so a child psychiatrist is more likely to start by prescribing an SSRI. SSRIs affect nerve cells in the brain that carry signals, and it makes serotonin more available to the body (Mayo Clinic, 2022c). Serotonin stabilizes the emotions in the body and increases feelings of calm and happiness.

There are common behavior modifications that can also assist the child. Social anxiety is not a curable condition, but it is very treatable. Teachers can assist with the treatment process. It is important to encourage children to participate in social activities but not to force them to participate, which can cause even more anxiety. Adults can also use compliments and praise when a child is able to handle a scary situation. It is important to not criticize a child for her fears. The important adults in the child's life need to remain supportive and show confidence in the child.

Case Study: Nora

Nora is an 11-year-old girl entering sixth grade. It is the end of the summer, and school is set to begin in a week. She has begun to tell her parents, "I hate going to school" and "I don't know if I can face it again this year." When her parents asked her about it, she said she dreaded answering questions in front of others and worried she would say something "stupid." She shared that in fourth grade a peer laughed at her when she blurted out a wrong answer to a math question. She felt humiliated.

She also shared with them that when she performed in the school play last year, she felt that her part was serious but she was convinced that others laughed at her. Her parents attended this play, and they did not have the same impression of her performance. In fact, her parents reminded her that she had a standing ovation for her part. Still, Nora is convinced that she "sounded dumb" in front of everyone.

At the end of her fifth-grade year, her parents noticed an increase in her absences, but they assumed she was burnt out and ready for summer. Nora is now saying she was absent from school because the thought of being in front of others at school and feeling judged by them was "unbearable." Her parents report feeling baffled because they did not know she was feeling so many emotions under the surface. To date, her parents have not had any concerning feedback from Nora's teachers, so they are assuming she is not noticeably distressed at school. Three weeks into her sixth-grade year, her parents decide to seek counseling for Nora to help her with her anxious thoughts and feelings regarding school, peers, and talking to others.

Her parents note that she was historically "slow to warm up" to strangers, but that is about it in terms of being fearful of others. She was an easy baby. In her toddler years, she attended child care, and once she knew the routine, she thrived. Her parents describe her as inquisitive and curious. She once took random ingredients out of the fridge to see if she could bake a cake "all by myself." This "cake" was more the consistency of a mudpie, but Nora felt proud of herself all the same.

In kindergarten through third grade, her parents did not notice concerning issues regarding her social life or school life. They saw her as a slightly shy child who became quite animated once she was comfortable. Nora often said to friends, "Just wait until you know me. I'm not so quiet!" Parents describe her school experience as positive, which is why this new feedback about "hating school" seems out of character for Nora. Her parents note that Nora has never had a large friend group, but she has consistently had good friends.

Nora vividly remembers blurting out a wrong answer in math class and her classmates laughing. She recounts this moment as feeling "punched in the stomach." She describes feeling her face flush and getting hot and sweaty. After this moment, she was more reluctant to answer questions in class. In addition, she began to believe that others were waiting for her to mess up again.

During summer camp, her parents noticed that if she needed to speak to someone she did not know, like a peer, she avoided it. She would politely read a book or appear to be "working hard" on something. This way of avoiding interacting with peers was new. Her parents noticed it on her swim team as well. She was aloof and often alone. She practiced her strokes and worked on her personal times, but she sat by herself when she was out of the water.

Nora's parents also noticed that she quit ordering for herself at restaurants. Instead of placing her own order, she began to have her little brother do it or she asked her parents to order for her. When they asked her why, she said that she feels embarrassed to have strangers hear her speak.

In the third week of sixth grade, Nora and her parents attended an intake therapy session. In this session, Nora disclosed that she now realizes when she missed school at the end of last year, she was avoiding feeling anxious with others. She also noted that once summer arrived, she so wanted the bad feelings to go away that she did not tell anyone about how she was feeling in fifth grade. It was only as she faced entering sixth grade, and the familiar sinking feeling in her stomach returned, that she realized a big problem was awaiting her.

Her therapy included CBT (how to unpair thoughts with their impact on her behavior) and helping her face her fears of being judged. Her parents were instrumental in helping her face her fears, as were her teachers at school.

Three months into school, Nora can report dreading school less. She is still not comfortable with being called on in class or speaking aloud in front of a group, but she can face going to school. At the beginning of sixth grade, she would anxiously stand outside the door of her classroom debating if she should walk in. Now she can practice "box breathing" before pushing the door open and will walk to her seat. She still hides behind books when she feels anxious, but she is slowly challenging that coping mechanism too. Nora reports feeling some hope, even though she is still scared.

Selective Mutism 5

Selective mutism is an anxiety disorder characterized by the child's inability to speak in certain settings, such as school; however, the child is capable of normal speech in a familiar setting, such as home (Selective Mutism Association, 2022). The child can speak, but the anxiety prevents him from speaking at times. Selective mutism usually begins between the ages of 2 and 4 years, when children begin interacting with others from outside their homes (Cleveland Clinic, 2022). The child freezes in a setting where he is expected to talk, and the panic prevents him from being able to speak at all. He may have frozen facial expressions or a look of panic on his face when someone speaks to him.

A child with selective mutism is typically comfortable speaking to family members. In fact, at home she may be chatty or boisterous. Each case of selective mutism may be slightly different. Some children will speak to immediate family members, but they will not speak to extended family members they do not see often. Most children with selective mutism will not speak at school; however, they may have one close friend with whom they will discreetly speak in the classroom. An adult outside the home may tell a child that it is rude to not speak when spoken to; however, this condition, closely linked to social anxiety, prevents the child from being able to speak regardless of the wishes of others.

Selective mutism is a very persistent condition, and it can last into adulthood if not treated. Statistics show that approximately 1 in 140 children are diagnosed with the condition (Selective Mutism Association, 2022). Females and children learning English as a second language are twice as likely to be diagnosed with selective mutism compared with the overall population. Also, of all children with selective mutism, 70% of them also have a diagnosis of social anxiety disorder. The normal duration of the condition is 8 years (ZERO TO THREE, 2016).

SYMPTOMS

The predominant characteristic of selective mutism is the difference in how the child communicates with familiar people compared to less familiar people. The frozen posture and facial features are also a characteristic sign of selective mutism. Any time the child is pushed outside of her comfort zone, the frozen demeanor will return. Selective mutism can be distinguished from a significant speech and language delay by the child's ability to interact freely with loved ones. The child may have some speech delays, but selective mutism is not noted as a condition based on the child's vocabulary or ability to articulate words (ASHA, 2022). Other symptoms may include the following:

- Appears shy or withdrawn
- Is clingy with parents in social settings
- Appears nervous and socially awkward
- Appears rude or disinterested
- Behaves in a stubborn or aggressive manner (may have a meltdown when continually questioned by adults)
- Appears to be expressionless or has a flat affect
- Struggles to make eye contact with others

A child with a milder case of selective mutism may feel comfortable giving someone a high-five or waving. More significant forms of selective mutism will prevent communication in all forms: gestures, written communication, and verbal communication (ASHA, 2022). Some children may occasionally whisper a few words, but it will depend on how comfortable they feel in a specific social setting.

A child with selective mutism may begin to show symptoms of academic challenges (Selective Mutism Association, 2022). Children with this diagnosis will not ask teachers clarifying questions when they do not understand an assignment or if they are confused about classroom directions. A child may be discouraged or insecure when a teacher asks another student to read a high-quality assignment out loud, knowing that the teacher will not ask them. It can be difficult for the teacher to assess a child's ability to read when he will not read aloud, so if the student is struggling, the teacher cannot assess the situation. It can also be challenging to assess speech and language delays when teachers or specialists cannot observe a child's speech patterns.

Although selective mutism does not normally have many physical symptoms, it can cause a child to have repetitive bladder infections (Selective Mutism Association, 2022). Often, a child with selective mutism will not even speak at school to ask to go to the restroom. This means that the child will have to wait for multiple hours to go to the restroom or may have an accident at school. It may not be obvious at first that the child is not asking to use the restroom until accidents or infections start. At that point, the teacher may have to create a way for the child to ask permission to use the bathroom without drawing too much attention. Older children may figure out that it is difficult to wait all day to use the bathroom, so they may not eat or drink at school in order to avoid asking.

Although many people with selective mutism are shy, there is a significant difference between shyness and selective mutism (Selective Mutism Association, 2022). Shyness is related to a child's temperament, and selective mutism is a mental health disorder. A shy child may not participate in group activities and withdraw from others, especially people the child has not interacted with before. Selective mutism prohibits the child from living a normal life, so it is much more significant. Shyness may naturally reduce over time, but selective mutism needs treatment in order for the child to make improvement. The stress of an anxiety disorder like selective mutism will not only affect a child's ability to interact with others, but also it can have a long-term negative impact on the child's education and eventual employment.

CAUSES

There is not a known cause for selective mutism. Selective mutism, along with other anxiety disorders, can run in families (ASHA, 2022). This means that some of the possible causes of more general anxiety disorders may be a factor. If the child has a speech and language challenge, such as stuttering, then it could make speaking more stressful and possibly lead to selective mutism. Children who have experienced abuse or trauma could also have selective mutism, but not all children who experience trauma display selective mutism. Some people may believe that selective mutism is a disability related to control and manipulation; however, because it is based on anxiety, the need for control is not an underlying cause for the diagnosis. There has also been no proven link between selective mutism and autism spectrum disorder, although it is possible for a child to have both conditions.

DIAGNOSIS

When a mental health professional is diagnosing selective mutism, she will look for several specific characteristics. First, the diagnosis includes a persistent failure to speak in social settings outside of the home despite the ability to speak (ZERO TO THREE, 2016). Another key characteristic is that the failure to speak is not related to a speech or language disorder that prevents the child from speaking, such as if the child were nonverbal. The diagnostician is also going to observe whether the child's inability to speak is having a significant impact on the child's life and on the family's life.

The diagnostician will ask about the child's family history and if there has been a previous pattern of selective mutism or other anxiety disorders with other family members (ASHA, 2022). It is also important for the diagnostician to know what language is typically spoken in the home and if it is the same language spoken at the child's school and in other social environments. A child with selective mutism may not speak to the adult doing the assessment, but the assessor may try to find a way for the child to communicate, such as drawing pictures. If the child will not speak directly to the mental health professional, then he or she will be prepared for that.

The diagnostician will also want to know about how the child communicates with family members and others to whom she is close (Selective Mutism Association, 2022). The specialist will ask the parents about their concerns about the child's behavior, and he or she will also ask about the length of time that the child has been exhibiting the frozen or panicked behaviors. The diagnostic process may include an assessment by a speech-language pathologist (ASHA, 2022). The speech-language pathologist will look at the function of the mouth, jaw, and tongue, and he or she will also try to rule out other speech and language disorders that may cause similar symptoms.

TREATMENTS

Selective mutism needs to be treated as an anxiety disorder and not as a speech and language disorder unless there are underlying speech problems that also need to be addressed (Selective Mutism Association, 2022). The treatment should not focus on how to speak, but instead it should focus on how to reduce the child's anxiety so that he or she can feel comfortable speaking in a social setting. The treatment team may involve a mental health professional and a speech-language pathologist. It is also important for the family to include the teacher and school in the treatment plan so that every important adult in the child's life is providing a consistent approach to treatment.

The treatment plan is likely to begin with cognitive-behavioral therapy (CBT) to help the child change the way he perceives himself and others around him (Cleveland Clinic, 2022). CBT is more appropriate for older children and adolescents. If a child is diagnosed with selective mutism in preschool, then she may start with play-based therapy. One of the main goals is to talk about the anxiety and how it affects the child's mind and body. It is also important to talk about coping strategies that the child can use to manage anxious behaviors.

Behavioral therapy may also be used. Instead of focusing on the anxiety, behavioral therapy focuses on creating new positive behaviors (ASHA, 2022). Some of the primary behavioral techniques used for selective mutism are graded exposure, stimulus fading, shaping, and desensitization. Graded exposure means exposing the child to the least stressful situation first in order to help him manage his anxiety level and develop coping skills. As the child's skill level grows, then he could be exposed to a slightly more complicated social situation. Stimulus fading also allows the child to slowly increase his skill level. The child starts off by talking with someone with whom he feels very comfortable, such as a parent. The next step is to introduce a slightly less familiar person into that situation while keeping the comfort of the parent still being present in the conversation.

Shaping is a behavioral therapy technique that allows a child to slowly modify his or her behavior to eventually produce the desired behavior (ASHA, 2022). For a young child, the goal may be to have him participate in a two-way conversation. The shaping process may begin with hearing his own voice read aloud, moving to a chanting game where multiple students speak out loud, and then eventually participate in a conversation with a peer. Desensitization is also a gradual process that allows the child to become accustomed to hearing his own voice out loud. This may start with picture or written communication to a peer and then move to speaking over a phone or in person.

Medication may or may not be needed, depending on the recommendation of a child psychiatrist or pediatrician. If the family chooses to place the child on medication, it is important for the teacher to document any medical or behavioral side effects that are visible in the classroom. Side effects can be an indication that the child may need a different type or dosage of the medication for it to be most effective.

Parent education or coaching classes can be very beneficial for the family to best support the child. There are several behavioral techniques that parents may be encouraged to remember while the child is receiving a multimodal form of treatment. Although the goal of the treatment is to help the child learn how to speak in public situations, it is important for the family to not put immense pressure on the child to speak. The pressure of pleasing a loved one may make the child even more anxious. Instead, it is important for the parents to tell the child that they understand it is hard for her to speak and that they know she is scared. Reassuring the child to take small steps when she is ready allows her to feel safety instead of pressure.

Parents can also encourage their child to use nonverbal communication, like high-fives or waving, if he or she is not yet comfortable speaking out loud. If the child is brave enough to speak out loud in a social setting, this is obviously something worth celebrating; however, to avoid embarrassment, a parent should not congratulate the child out loud in a social setting. It is better to acknowledge the child's bravery in a private conversation.

The family does not need to avoid social settings to alleviate the child's anxiety. It is appropriate to attend events that are part of the family's normal routine. When at the event, it may help to assist the child in finding strategies to cope with the social setting. The parents may also want to ask friends and family to give the child the opportunity to warm up to the new environment before all greeting her at one time and asking her questions.

The most important strategy for parents is to be patient and remember that this is a slow process. Because the goal is to reduce the child's anxiety and help her feel safe enough to be social with others, building a loving and safe environment for the child is key.

Case Study: Akio

Akio is a "shy" 6-year-old Japanese American boy. He lives with his parents and grandparents. His parents are bilingual (Japanese and English), but his grandparents speak limited English. Japanese is the primary language spoken in his home so that everyone can communicate easily. Akio is also bilingual and can switch easily between Japanese and English.

In his home, Akio is lively and talkative, but the moment he leaves his front door, he becomes silent. His physical presence also changes when he leaves his house: he rounds his shoulders and avoids eye contact. He is isolated in his world outside of his house because he remains silent. This interferes with his ability to make and maintain friendships, as well as having an impact on his academics. His anxiety about using his voice outside of his home has been growing. The less he uses his voice, the more frightened he has become of others hearing him speak.

Akio was born premature at 30 weeks old. He needed to be cared for in the pediatric intensive care unit for the first weeks of his life. As he gained weight and learned to breastfeed and bottle feed, he was discharged to his parents' care. His parents describe him as a sweet and easygoing baby. He would cry if uncomfortable but otherwise seemed content.

Akio enjoyed playing in his house and in the backyard. He was quite imaginative and would spend hours creating pretend worlds full of characters and story lines. Akio would happily play and talk with his cousin when he visited. They would spend hours creating forts and playing games together.

When Akio turned 4, his parents enrolled him in a child care program that transitions into his local elementary school. At this time, his parents were aware that when Akio ran errands with them, he would become "shy." He would not answer if an adult spoke to him, and he would avoid eye contact. His parents were not particularly worried because this can be a normal response for a young child.

During the first child care conference with Akio's parents, his teachers shared that he is a joy to have in class but that he also avoids eye contact and does not speak to anyone in his classroom. He happily plays during free time and listens during instruction, but if he is asked a question, he simply does not respond. His parents agreed to work with him at home on trying to talk to others outside of the home. He was able to learn and keep up with his peers in child care. He even made a friend who did not seem to mind Akio playing silently beside him. He reported liking school. When his parents asked, "Why do you not want to talk at school?" Akio would simply look at his parents and not answer.

Akio's silence persisted in his kindergarten year. He maintained his friendship with his one peer but otherwise played alone. He continued to avoid eye contact. He did not utter a word to his teacher for the first half of the year. During the second semester, he developed enough trust with his teacher to whisper "yes" or "no" to questions, although he did not always answer when asked a question. His parents felt baffled that he could speak so freely and have strong opinions at home but remained silent at school. He managed to keep up academically in kindergarten. His classmates were used to him not speaking, so it did not really affect his functioning that much.

In first grade, as the academic work became more challenging, Akio began to struggle. His one friend moved away during the summer of kindergarten, and he was more isolated than before. Akio reverted to not speaking at all at school. He would not answer "yes" or "no" questions anymore. Akio's parents and teachers decided to do some interventions to see whether they could help him feel safe at school. They involved his kindergarten teacher because he had spoken with her in the past. They also agreed to enroll him in play therapy to see whether a nonverbal form of therapy could help him communicate safely outside of his home.

When his therapist met him for the first time, she led him to the sand tray. He had access to both wet and dry sand as well as hundreds of tiny figures. She introduced herself and gave him freedom to explore the sand and toys however he wanted. He did not speak, nor did he look at her. She noted that he appeared vaguely aware of her presence; however, if she adjusted in her seat, his eyes quickly darted to her to see what she was doing. It became clear that he was keenly aware of her presence and even anxious about her presence. When spoken to, Akio looked up or made eye contact. He would play.

Over time, he began engaging in parallel play in therapy sessions. He would tolerate his therapist playing with a figure in the sand tray with him. It took 3 months of weekly therapy sessions before Akio made eye contact with his therapist. As this happened, his therapist began to ask him, "Can your eyes find my eyes?" He would usually comply for a second with this request. At 6 months of therapy, Akio had created a game he loved to play in therapy…hide and seek. There were few hiding spots, but he would create them with blankets and pillows. When his therapist "found" him, he would giggle in a silent, breathy giggle. He still did not vocalize. However, trust was being built in his world.

By the end of the school year, Akio was speaking to his kindergarten and first-grade teachers using one-word answers. He also began to do this with a few of his classmates. He continued to be animated and talkative at home. His academics were still lagging, but he was able to move on to second grade. The plan for the summer was to have him enroll in a social skills group and tutoring all summer as well as to continue his play therapy sessions. His team agreed to reassess his needs in the fall and see what growth he made over the summer.

Obsessive-Compulsive Disorder   6

Obsessive-compulsive disorder (OCD) is a condition where negative thoughts and worries consistently prevent a child from leading a normal life. Instead of worrying about a test or speaking in front of the class, the child worries about performing rituals and specific actions to prevent bad things from happening. When a negative thought enters a child's head, the child feels that he must take some sort of action to make the thought go away, even if the action is completely irrational (CDC, 2022b). This may mean that a child believes that she must wear a certain color shirt or repeat a chant to prevent something bad from happening. These thoughts take up so much time that it is hard for the child to carry on with a normal day. The thoughts are known as obsessions because the child focuses on them so consistently. The actions that the children take to control the thoughts (e.g., cleaning, chanting) are the compulsions.

There is a misconception that OCD means that the child is very focused on cleaning and organizing. That is one possible behavior that can be demonstrated with OCD; however, other children may be very focused on an obsession and want to do it over and over again to calm their anxiety. An example of this is clicking the lights on and off a certain number of times before leaving a room. It is also possible for the child's obsession to change over time.

Children with OCD continually worry about unrealistic and unrelated consequences. They must continue to complete their compulsive rituals to have any sense of temporary relief. If a parent interrupts the child's ritual in order to calm him down, then the child will completely stop and start the ritual over so that it can be done according to his standard. The child may allow the parent to participate in the ritual, but he will find it unacceptable for the parent to disrupt the ritual.

SYMPTOMS

When a child has OCD, she may show signs of obsessions, compulsions, or both (CDC, 2022b). So, instead of just one list of symptoms that the child may show for a different anxiety disorder, OCD has a list of both obsessions and compulsions that a child may demonstrate. There are some compulsions, or actions, that seem to directly pair with the obsessions (negative thoughts); however, the child may not demonstrate both.

Here is a potential list of obsessions:

- Fear of dirt and germs
- Fear of touching surfaces with dirt and germs
- Fear and doubts about household safety, including locked doors and closed windows
- Fear of getting hurt
- Fear of hurting a family member or friend
- Obsession over appearance or organization (e.g., arranging the bedroom in a certain way, drawing a picture that is perfectly symmetrical, only wearing certain clothes)
- Fears or superstitions that something bad will happen if the child does not do something completely unrelated in order to stop the negative action (e.g., stepping on a crack, throwing salt over the shoulder, tapping on a hard surface)

If a child displays compulsions, it is possible to see the following:

- A constant desire to wash, bathe, or put on clean clothes
- A desire to constantly repeat words, chants, or prayers to prevent bad things from happening
- Inflexibility regarding morning and evening routines
- Physical rituals where the child moves her body in symmetrical or patterned movements
- Seeking continuous reassurance from parents, teachers, and other loved ones
- Trying to avoid any environment where something bad could occur

When a mental health specialist is looking at the symptoms present for a diagnosis, there are several key characteristics that must be demonstrated. Again, it is not necessary for a child to show both obsessive and compulsive behaviors in order to receive the diagnosis. At least one of the two behaviors must be observed, but frequently both behaviors are displayed (ZERO TO THREE, 2016). Also, the behaviors must occur almost every day and consume a great deal of the child's time. The obsessions and compulsions cannot be attributed to any other medical condition or mental health disorder, such as autism spectrum disorder or trichotillomania. The obsessions and compulsions should not be linked specifically to a traumatic event.

As with many of the anxiety-based disorders diagnosed at a young age, the diagnosing specialist needs to observe that the severity of the condition is limiting the child's and the family's ability to live a normal life. The condition needs to be present for at least 3 months before diagnosis (ZERO TO THREE, 2016). Also, infants and toddlers are not diagnosed with this condition. Preschool-age children and elementary students are more likely to be diagnosed with OCD, and more cases are diagnosed in older children. Younger onset of OCD has been associated with a comorbidity of other anxiety disorders or a diagnosis of attention-deficit/hyperactivity disorder.

CAUSES

OCD could have multiple causes. The most common possibilities are genetics, environment, and the biology of the brain (Mayo Clinic, 2022a). There is some research that OCD could be a genetically linked trait; however, at this time, no gene has been isolated to prove that theory. Individual brain chemistry and function could also be a contributing factor to cause OCD. Similar to an illness like epilepsy, the way that the brain functions allows for the tendencies of OCD to live successfully within the brain. The environment is a major factor in OCD as well. When a child grows up in a home where an adult is already diagnosed with OCD, the child learns to model the coping mechanisms of the adults with whom they live.

TRIGGERS

A trigger for an increase in OCD behavior could be based on general mental health risk factors or it could be linked to the individual obsession. When we think about general triggers, the most common are stressful life events, other mental health disorders, big life changes (e.g., birth of a sibling, moving to a new house, starting a new school), or experiencing trauma. Many of these types of events make the child or adolescent feel out of control. Because OCD is an anxiety disorder with accompanying action steps, completing the compulsions may help the patient feel more control.

It is also possible for an individual obsession to be triggered. For example, a child who is obsessed with being clean may be triggered by having to use a public toilet or participating in messy play at school. That same child could be triggered by simply being in an environment that requires close physical contact with others so that she must hug or shake hands with lots of people, potentially contaminating her clean hands.

A child who is obsessed with thinking about himself or his family getting hurt could be triggered by hearing about a neighborhood house fire or hearing a story in the news about a car wreck or airplane crash. The same child could be triggered even more by a death in the family or harm coming to someone that he knows personally. When a child demonstrates

an increase in obsessive and compulsive behavior, it is important for the teachers and the parents to communicate to see what type of life events the family may be going through that may have spurred the increasingly anxious behaviors. It is also important to remember that if the child was affected by something as common as a news story, the family may not even know that the child heard that type of information, so there may be no obvious reason for the change in behavior.

TREATMENTS

To start the treatment process for OCD, most medical professionals will recommend cognitive-behavioral therapy (CBT) and medication. Again, CBT is a type of talk therapy that allows the child to look at his feelings and behaviors and then develop tools to deal with his anxiety in a more successful way. There is one specific type of CBT that is often recommended for patients with OCD. It is called *exposure and response prevention (ERP)*, and it helps the child gradually resist using the compulsive behaviors (Mayo Clinic, 2022a). Although the child may not completely stop using the compulsive behaviors, this type of treatment can help him limit the negative impacts the behaviors can have.

The most common type of medication treatment for OCD is a selective serotonin reuptake inhibitor (SSRI). SSRIs positively affect the brain by slowing down the reabsorption of serotonin in the brain. This allows serotonin to build up between the neurons and improve the way the brain sends messages. Overall, an SSRI reduces the anxiety level in the brain, and then CBT can help the child learn how to process the anxiety that remains.

Not all cases of OCD can be improved with medication. There is a type of OCD known as treatment-resistant OCD. This condition will not be diagnosed until a patient has been on an SSRI for at least 12 weeks to make sure the body has adjusted to the new medication

(NIMH, 2022). The doctor will also want to try at least one other SSRI to make sure that the child is not just having side effects from that particular medication. Treatment-resistant OCD cases are rare, but they are significant. They may require inpatient treatment or more advanced medical procedures to help the child be more successful at controlling the compulsive behaviors.

Frequently, a therapist will also work with the parents of the child in order to help them use correct behavior strategies in the home. It is essential that a parent does not allow a child to avoid all her fears. The parent should not open doors for the child so that she does not have to touch a dirty doorknob. When it comes to fears the child encounters each day, such as opening doors, the parent should allow the child to face the fear and help her problem-solve her way through it. At the same time, the parent should not intentionally expose the child to extra stressors to help her learn how to deal with them. This elevated level of stress can cause the child to regress and show even more compulsive behaviors.

It is also important for parents and teachers to remember that the child is not being defiant on purpose. She feels a need to demonstrate the compulsive behaviors as soon as the obsessive thoughts begin to occur. If a parent or teacher tells the child to stop, she may not have the mental or physical control to stop the process in the middle of her routine. If she does stop, she will often be compelled to start the process over from the beginning. This is not an act of defiant behavior, so it is important that the adults in the child's life practice patience as the treatment process begins.

Case Study: Emily

Emily is a 7-year-old girl in first grade. She and her parents are seeking consultation to help Emily interrupt several OCD cleaning rituals that stem from a fear of germs. Her symptoms worsened during the COVID-19 pandemic because Emily fears she could be contaminated or contaminate her loved ones with germs. She uses hand sanitizer excessively and cleans her desk at school multiple times daily. She has begun to walk with her hands pressed to her sides, as if glued down, so her hands do not touch germy surfaces. She has also begun to decline being hugged by friends or family members. When asked, she will say, "I just don't like hugs."

Emily's parents report that her fear of germs surfaced when COVID-19 emerged and her school was closed during her kindergarten year. When her school reopened, she attended first grade, and this is when her cleaning rituals became very noticeable. Her peers were initially curious about all her different hand sanitizers, but Emily would not speak about it to them. She simply pretended that she did not hear them. As this continued, Emily became more isolated from her friends. At the time of therapy, Emily feels that she does not have as many close friendships as she did in kindergarten. Her hands are dry from all the sanitizer, but in the intake session, she notices the sanitizer on the desk and begins to use it repeatedly. She becomes quiet when the therapist asks why she feels she needs to use the sanitizer after she just used it, but she responds, "I don't want to get sick from germs because I could give it to others, and they could die." Emily's parents are supportive and open to seeking counseling. Both report feeling helpless when they see Emily engage in cleaning rituals.

As an infant, she needed to be soothed by constant rocking or movement. When she was still, she would cry in distress. She avoided loud noises and cried if something unexpected happened (e.g., a balloon being popped). Her parents were able to soothe her, but it took a lot of energy. As a toddler, her parents were amused at her enjoyment at arranging and organizing her toys. They described her as more difficult to soothe in infancy, but she was a bit more easygoing as a toddler unless the daily schedule was changed. For instance, if a babysitter needed to come over, she would cry and follow her parents around the house. Her parents liked to joke that she was like "a little adult" in terms of her organizational skills. She enjoyed spending time lining up toys and helping her parents with simple household tasks.

Emily struggled when her parents left her with a babysitter, so her parents were also anxious when her first day of kindergarten arrived. During the car ride, Emily excitedly asked many questions about her teachers, when she would be picked up, and who would pick her up from school. Her parents answered each question several times. When she got to school, she clung to her mom and cried. She did not want to make eye contact with her teacher or peers. Eventually, her teacher coaxed her to sit by another little girl, and her parents left. Emily developed a ritual to help her feel safe to leave her parents and transition to school: she would ask her parents the same questions three times each, share a special handshake with her parent, and wait for her friend to walk into class together.

Her parents were relieved that she found a way to manage getting into the classroom, even though it felt tiring to watch her go to such lengths to feel safe. In her kindergarten year, her teachers described her as observant and kind to peers. She found two friends at school and did not venture out to play with other children as much, but she reported enjoying school. At parent–teacher conferences, her teachers spoke of her intelligence and ability to follow directions as being particularly strong.

As COVID-19 hit, Emily seemed content to stay at home and not be challenged to leave her parent's side each day. She flourished in her predictable environment. She worked on school projects, made art, and had limited contact with peers. As summer ended and a new school year began, she expressed worry to her parents about becoming sick with COVID-19. Her parents educated her about mask protocols and handwashing. The night before first grade, Emily packed her new school supplies, complete with a variety of hand sanitizers and sanitizing wipes. She had her parents check her supplies list with her that night. The next morning, she wanted to recheck that she had all of her supplies, and then she went to school.

She practiced the same ritual of asking questions as she did the previous year, but she felt a bit more prepared to leave her parents. At the end of each night, her parents noticed that she wiped down her backpack with a sanitizing wipe and checked that she had all of her supplies ready for the next day. She did the same cleaning ritual the next morning. She would wipe all zippers, handles, and surfaces of her backpack. She would also excessively clean her water bottle. When parents asked her about these cleaning rituals, she would become defensive and say, "I'm just keeping things germ free." Her parents sensed that a lot more was going on than "just being germ free," so they sought her teacher's feedback.

Her teacher shared that each morning Emily was pulling a hand towel out of her backpack and placing it on her desk chair. She would spend time arranging it so that all edges of the chair were covered. Then she would go to the teacher's desk to grab a sanitizing wipe and clean the surface of her desk. Finally, she would use hand sanitizer on her hands. Throughout the day, Emily would repeat adjusting the hand towel followed by cleaning her hands. Her teacher shared that the routine was noticeable to the other kids, and she was concerned about how it was impacting Emily's friendships. Her parents reported feeling scared for their daughter.

In this case, Emily was already developing signs of pediatric OCD, but the event of the COVID-19 pandemic complicated Emily's fear of germs. She had an unreasonable amount of fear of germs, but it was difficult for her parents to challenge because it was an actual community threat.

In OCD, often the child may know that the amount of fear they experience is not reasonable, but it is so uncomfortable that they persist in the compulsive behaviors to alleviate their fear. In this case, Emily would rather have her friends think her handwashing is "weird" than worry that she could have life-threatening germs. She would rather have her parents be sad about not getting a hug than risk giving COVID-19 to someone. Instead of allowing herself to play freely, she preferred to control her hands and keep them at her sides so she could feel less contaminated. Instead of sitting like her peers, she felt that she had to use a towel to keep her skin and clothing free from germs. In Emily's mind, the threat was so strong that it was worth risking upsetting others to protect herself and others from the feared outcome.

The thoughts are so distressing that the person feels compelled (must do something) to alleviate the distress inside the body. Unfortunately, this strengthens the cycle of OCD. The more Emily attempted to clean and organize her world, the more she allowed her distressing thoughts to control her actions. In Emily's case, her therapy consisted of three components: medication management with her physician, exposure and response prevention CBT, and parent/teacher coaching.

Childhood Phobias 7

C hildhood phobias are another type of anxiety, but they are much more specific than many of the anxiety-based conditions. A phobia is a very intense fear that can even cause a child to experience dread. The phobia can be about a person, an animal or an insect, an object, a situation, or a place. The phobia can cause a child to avoid the feeling of fear at all costs, or it could cause the child to experience sheer terror when he encounters the object of his fear. A phobia is so intense that even reassurance from a parent will not let that fear subside. The phobia can cause the child to dread his fear even when he is not around it.

Of course, all children have fears. Fears are completely normal for typically developing children. Each age range has fears that are most common for the development of the child (WebMD, 2022):

Infants and Toddlers

- Loud noises
- Looming objects
- Sudden movements
- Strangers
- Separation from a loved one
- Falling (e.g., startle reflex)

Preschool-Age Children

- The dark
- Monsters
- Noises at night
- People wearing medical masks or costume masks
- Animals like dogs
- Snakes and spiders
- Shots at the doctor's office
- Storms and natural disasters

School-Age Children

- Scary news and TV shows
- Illness and injury
- Doctors, shots, and blood
- Snakes and spiders
- Storms and natural disasters
- A teacher or important adult who is angry
- Being home alone
- Fire drills
- Burglars
- War
- Failure or rejection

Younger children fear pretend things (Nemours Children's Health, 2022b). Older children fear real-life dangers, and adolescents have social fears. Most children move through stages of having these fears. The fear transitions to a phobia when it lasts for a significant amount of time (a minimum of 6 months) and it begins to affect a child's ability to participate in normal childhood activities.

Up to 10% of children have one phobia or more (Boston Children's Hospital, 2022b). As children grow out of some typical childhood fears, there are certain phobias that tend to stay with children longer than others. The most common childhood phobias include the following, which are categorized by intense fear and a predominant emphasis in the child's life.

- **Acrophobia—the intense fear of heights:** A child does not have to be far off the ground to experience this phobia. Even the thought of falling from a height would be enough to cause a strong reaction.

- **Arachnophobia—the fear of spiders:** This fear is so intense and irrational that a child will imagine spiders even when they are not present. The child may avoid going certain places in order to avoid contact with spiders.

- **Astraphobia—the fear of storms:** This child is not only afraid of storms but may also obsessively watch weather reports or have panic attacks during storms.

- **Aviophobia—the fear of flying:** A child can be afraid to simply get on a plane, let alone fly on the plane. The fear may also cause nightmares as soon as the child realizes that he may have to fly on a plane.

- **Claustrophobia—the fear of enclosed spaces:** This phobia can make a child afraid of getting on an elevator, getting on an airplane, or entering a crowded room. It can also affect children if they have to be in an enclosed space such as an MRI machine. The phobia can cause the child to avoid participation in group activities.

- **Cynophobia—the extreme fear of dogs:** Children with this phobia will go out of their way to avoid any interaction with dogs. Simply hearing a dog bark can induce a great deal of fear.

- **Hemophobia—the fear of blood:** This phobia includes the fear of seeing any blood, including seeing blood from someone else getting injured. It also includes a fear of getting medical tests or shots. This phobia can have a significant impact on a person's life if it prevents her from receiving necessary medical treatment.

- **Nosophobia—the fear of getting sick:** Individuals with this phobia are constantly worried about getting sick. This was once called hypochondriasis. A child with nosophobia is very worried about any change in the body and is convinced he is getting sick.

- **Nyctophobia—the fear of darkness:** Fear of the dark will limit a child's activities, cause a child to avoid normal situations, and create fear when simply anticipating the loss of light.

- **Ophidiophobia—the fear of snakes:** This phobia is much more than a simple fear. The individual is not only afraid of seeing or touching a snake but also is afraid to even discuss the topic of snakes.

SYMPTOMS

Every child with a phobia may have slightly different symptoms, but the symptoms can include both emotional and physical symptoms (Nemours Children's Health, 2022b). Most children will experience one or two symptoms, like an increased heart rate or increased sweating. If a child begins to experience four or more symptoms at once, then it is probable that he is having a panic attack. Just like other medical conditions, a panic attack should be reported to a medical professional. Most panic attacks subside after 10 minutes. If the panic attack lasts longer than that, it is also important to contact a medical professional.

Symptoms of a phobia can include:

- Increasing heart rate
- Sweating
- Shortness of breath
- Upset stomach
- Trembling or shaking
- Dizziness or feeling faint
- A choking feeling
- Chest pain or discomfort
- Chills or hot flashes
- Numbness

- Fear of losing control
- Fear of dying

An individual phobia may have more specific symptoms (Boston Children's Hospital, 2022b). If the child is afraid of dogs, then she will exhibit symptoms more specific to dogs. She will try to avoid dogs at all costs. She will anticipate seeing dogs and dread the moment when she finally encounters them. She will also spend so much time fearing dogs and thinking about them, that it can alter all her normal routines and even affect her relationships with others.

Although there is a long list of symptoms for phobias, it can be very difficult to diagnose a phobia since the symptoms can mimic many other anxiety conditions. The key for most mental health professionals is to look at the isolated types of fears that the child demonstrates. If the child seems to have many different types of phobias, then it may actually be a larger category of anxiety disorder. If the child has several phobias all related to social situations, then the child may have social anxiety. It is also important for the diagnostician to keep in mind how long the child has shown the symptoms of the phobia. A phobia means that the fear has been present for at least 6 months (Nemours Children's Health, 2022b). If the fear lasts a shorter amount of time, it may be just a development stage the child is passing through.

CAUSES

A phobia is a type of anxiety disorder, so the causes for a phobia are going to be similar to other anxiety disorders. Anxiety disorders can be caused by biological reasons, family history, or environmental reasons. The biological reasons can be created by an imbalance of serotonin and dopamine, two neurotransmitters that send messages back and forth in the brain. Serotonin regulates behavior and breathing, and dopamine regulates pleasure and satisfaction. When those two chemicals are out of balance, a child's anxiety level can easily increase.

A family history is another reason a child can have anxiety (Boston's Children Hospital, 2022b). Anxiety can be an inherited trait. The same way that a child might inherit blonde hair from a parent, a predisposition for anxiety can also be inherited. A child can also develop a tendency for anxiety by living in a home where the parents or caregiver demonstrate anxious behaviors. Children learn by example, so if they see adults cope with stressful situations in an anxious way, then they will learn those behaviors also.

Environmental factors, like a traumatic experience, can also cause children to experience anxiety. Once a child has experienced trauma, simply the thought of experiencing that event again can cause the anxiety to begin. Trauma is not the only life experience that can cause anxiety. Sometimes major life events, like moving to a new house or the arrival of a new sibling, can also cause anxiety until the child develops a new routine and knows what to expect. Recurring events, like starting a new school year, can also bring on anxiety until a child learns to deal with the changes to his routine.

As a child gets older and begins to worry more about what others think, embarrassment can be a factor that brings on a great deal of anxiety. Anxiety can occur if he anticipates that he could be embarrassed by an upcoming situation. Older children and adolescents will begin to avoid potentially embarrassing situations no matter what. Some younger children become aware of social attention at a young age, so they may also want to avoid embarrassment at any cost.

TREATMENTS

Treatment of a phobia will depend on the age of the child and the severity of the phobia. A preschool-age child would need to start with play-based therapy to help the child identify what is causing her fear. As a child gets older, then she could begin cognitive-behavioral therapy (CBT) to learn how to control the anxiety when it occurs. Whether the child receives play-based therapy or CBT, therapy must be utilized on a consistent basis. If the child only attends therapy erratically, it will be hard for her to make progress toward controlling her anxiety.

Depending on how the child's phobia affects the family as a whole, family therapy may also be recommended. Even if the family does not want counseling on how the phobia affects the others in the household, the parents might still want parent coaching on how to help the child reduce his anxiety. The staff at the child's school may also need information on how to support the child when his anxiety arises at school. The communication between the family and the school is essential to make sure that the child's support system is consistent. The family must initiate this collaboration, since medical and mental health information is confidential. Once the family opens the door for the partnership, the school needs to work on constant communication in order to help the child be as successful as possible.

It is possible that the family may choose to use medication as part of the treatment process. When a child is young, most families only choose to use medication if the level of anxiety is so high that it makes it difficult for the child to function. If the family chooses to use medication to help the child, then it is best practice to let the school know so that the teachers can be on the lookout for side effects from the medication. Side effects of the medication can vary, but they can include headaches, nausea, drowsiness, dry mouth, insomnia, dizziness, or nervousness. If the teacher notices the child showing these side effects, he should share this information with the family as soon as possible. It is possible that the child is not taking the correct dosage of the medication or that the child needs a different type of medication.

When the mental health professional begins to coach the family on how to support the child, she may suggest multiple strategies for the family to try. First, the family needs to be supportive of the child's fears and not attempt to shame the child for how he fears. Many children will already be embarrassed about their anxiety, so additional pressure from the family can intensify that problem. It is also essential that the family makes it a high priority to attend all of the child's therapy sessions and help implement those strategies in the home. Without follow-up on the advice offered from the therapists, it will take the child much longer to learn how to reduce his anxiety level.

Parents also need to help the child feel safe. Reassuring the child that the home is safe and she is loved can offer the assurance the child needs as a foundation on which to build coping skills. Once the child begins to feel comfortable talking about her feelings, then it is essential for parents and other loved ones to be there to listen to the child. Allowing her to verbalize her thoughts about the anxiety can help her identify what triggers her fears and how to handle them when they occur.

It is important that parents do not force their children to be exposed to their fears (Nemours Children's Health, 2022b). Natural exposure to the fear will allow the child time to begin learning to cope with the fear. At the same time, the triggers to some fears need to be reduced. If a child has nightmares about monsters or scary movies, then he might not be mature enough yet to watch those types of programs. Young children who are afraid of the dark can be reassured by having a consistent, soothing bedtime routines. If the child knows what to expect each evening, then turning off the lights at the end of bedtime preparations will not seem as overwhelming.

If a child is afraid of strangers or new places, then it is appropriate to slowly introduce a child to those settings with a loved one present until she feels safe enough to talk to someone on her own (Nemours Children's Health, 2022b). If she is successful at overcoming a fear one day or controlling her anxiety, then it is important to acknowledge that brave behavior and encourage her to do it again. A child may be able to practice coping responses at home by drawing pictures or using stuffed animals to act out the situation. This type of tool can help prepare a child for real-life exposure to anxiety.

Parents may have questions about if it is possible to prevent a phobia. There is no evidence that phobias can be avoided, but the best possible treatment for phobias is to start treatment as early as possible. A child may continue to struggle with the phobia for some time, but treatment can significantly reduce the child's anxiety. There will be times when it is harder for the child to control her fears, but consistent treatment will keep it under control as best as possible.

Anxiety and Childhood Trauma   8

Many children experience anxiety due to genetic reasons or a predisposition to anxiety due to their temperament, but some children experience anxiety because of past trauma. Previous exposure to violence, significant loss, disaster, medical trauma, or abuse can cause a child continued anxiety that the situation may surface again or from reliving the memories of the previous trauma. A child may experience trauma firsthand, but there can also be devastating effects from watching or hearing someone else experience trauma (ZERO TO THREE, 2016). Whether the trauma has happened to the child or the child watched someone else experience it, the same type of fear-based response is present. Other children may withdraw and become unresponsive to protect themselves from these terrible experiences. Children feel overwhelmed and helpless by these life-altering events.

There is not a specific way to define traumatic events. There are different types of trauma, and every child is going to react to trauma. For example, for a young child to experience her parents getting divorced is a traumatic event. Divorce divides the two primary caregivers and places them in two different homes. The child suddenly spends significantly less time with each caregiver, who are two of the most important people in the child's life. If the parents argue a great deal during and after the divorce, then the child experiences additional stress. She may not have any access to one parent when she is in the other parent's care (e.g., unable to talk on the phone and say goodnight). She may now have two distinctly different worlds with different homes, different friends, different places of worship, and different neighborhoods, and she is expected to transition between these two different realities with ease, possibly several times per week.

It is expected that all young children will struggle emotionally when their parents get divorced. There are concerns about children feeling unloved and abandoned, particularly if one parent is no longer involved in the children's lives. Despite the anguish of a divorce, some children can grieve over the loss and then regroup, whereas other children struggle for a much longer period. It is very difficult to predict how much a child will be affected by a divorce prior to the event. Sometimes, a child who appears to be well adjusted will struggle a great deal from a divorce. It may be the most traumatic event that the family has ever experienced, and the child has not had to develop additional coping skills until that point. Other children may generally have a harder time coping with change, but the caregivers are collaborating to make sure that the transition is as easy on the children as possible. This can help the children process the event and deal more quickly with their emotions.

WHAT ARE TRAUMATIC EVENTS?

A traumatic event is a scary, violent, or dangerous event that happens to a child. It can also be an event that happens to someone close to the child and the child witnesses the event. The event causes the child to fear for his own safety or the safety of a loved one. After the event, there are feelings of loss, helplessness, or stress. These strong emotions can often be triggered when the child is frustrated that he could not stop the event from happening. The child may react with high levels of stress that continue for some time, and eventually that elevated stress level can affect the child emotionally, physically, and mentally.

Another term for traumatic events is *adverse childhood experiences* (ACEs). The Centers for Disease Control and Prevention (CDC) and the Kaiser Permanente Health Care Organization did the original research in 1995 on the types of adverse or traumatic events that children are most likely to experience in the home (CDC, 2022a). There were several key points identified in the study. First, ACEs are more common than expected. Approximately two thirds of children experience at least one ACE while growing up, and about 40% of children experience two ACEs. The second key finding was that the more ACEs a child experiences, the poorer outcomes that individual may encounter later in life. These outcomes include depression, substance abuse, heart disease, diabetes, obesity, absences from school or work, and even earlier ages of death.

These are the top 10 ACEs:

1. Physical abuse
2. Sexual abuse
3. Verbal abuse

4. Physical neglect
5. Emotional neglect
6. Living with a family member who is diagnosed with a mental illness
7. Living with a family member who is addicted to alcohol or another substance
8. Having a family member in prison
9. Witnessing a parent being abused
10. Losing a parent to separation, divorce, or death

All children have the potential to experience an ACE, but certain groups of children have risks factors that make them more susceptible to experience an ACE. Those risk factors include the following:

- Families with low income
- Families with young parents or single parents
- Families with low levels of education
- Families with parents who were abused as children
- Families with high stress levels due to income
- Families who have a child with a disability or a chronic illness
- Families where a parent has lost a job
- Families with food insecurity and unstable housing
- Families where a parent does not understand child development or appropriate expectations for young children
- Families that are accepting of violence or aggression
- Families that are isolated and not connected with a community

TOXIC STRESS

The study on ACEs showed that the more ACEs a child experiences, the higher her stress level will be. If a child experiences a higher number of ACEs for an ongoing time period, then she may experience something called toxic stress. In the early 2000s, after research about ACEs had been published, the National Scientific Council on the Developing Child came up with the term *toxic stress* (Harvard Health Publishing, 2018). Toxic stress is when the child's mind and regulatory systems live in a sense of high alert for an extended period of time due to the level of trauma the child is experiencing. This can include the child's brain and the hormones that it produces during an emergency, but it can also include the immune system, the metabolic system, and the cardiovascular system. When the brain and the systems of the body operate on high alert for an extended period, it can cause damage to the vital organs as well as the child's emotional supports.

Toxic stress can look different in different children. Often, a child will show behavioral changes that could include irritability, withdrawal, difficulties interacting with peers, problems eating or sleeping, problems with bladder and bowel control, acting younger than his

age, or poor performance in school. Toxic stress can also be the underlying characteristic in other mental health diagnoses such as posttraumatic stress disorder (PTSD), attachment disorder, or deterioration of physical health (ZERO TO THREE, 2016).

POSTTRAUMATIC STRESS DISORDER

PTSD occurs when a child still has unresolved issues with past trauma. Not everyone who experiences trauma develops PTSD. Only between 3% and 15% of girls and 1% and 6% of boys develop PTSD after a traumatic event (CDC, 2022a). The child who does experience PTSD will frequently relive the traumatic event over and over again in his head. He may begin to fear it so much that he begins to avoid certain settings or activities that may remind him of the trauma. Other young children may act out their traumatic event through dramatic play or art because they think about the event so frequently. Because the trauma is so present in the child's mind, he may be constantly on the lookout for similar situations to occur. It may even seem that he is constantly looking for something bad to happen, when in all reality he is focusing on finding ways to protect himself no matter what situation should arise.

Children who have PTSD may display the following symptoms:

- Aggression
- Anxiety
- Depression
- Fear
- Avoidance

- Withdrawal
- Low self-esteem
- Difficulty making and keeping friends
- Feeling isolated
- Flashbacks or nightmares
- Destructive or risky behavior

ATTACHMENT DISORDERS

If childhood trauma was caused by someone the child loved, then it can have a significant impact on the child's ability to make and keep attached relationships. Attachment occurs when a young child can secure a bond with a caregiver. That attached relationship teaches the child that the caregiver will keep her safe, feed her, and meet all her basic needs. The child then learns that she can trust the caregiver, and the attached relationship begins. Once the child is able to establish a pattern of attached relationships with important caregivers such as the parents, the child care providers, and other significant adults in her life, then the framework is in place for that child to move forward with other trusting relationships in the future.

Attachment trauma can happen when the loving adult in the child's life is the source of the trauma. Once the child associates that adult with the trauma, then the child may attempt to run away or avoid the adult to prevent additional trauma. If the child recognizes that she can no longer trust an adult who was extremely important to her, then she may begin to reevaluate other relationships and worry whether the trauma could occur in that relationship as well. The trauma could be as significant as abuse, but a child may also experience attachment trauma over something like a divorce where she is angry with her parents for breaking their home apart. Potential causes for attachment trauma could include a loss in the family, neglect, abuse, divorce, a caregiver with a mental illness, a caregiver with a substance abuse disorder, domestic violence, a caregiver who is not emotionally available to the child, or a caregiver who attempts to control all of the child's behaviors.

As a child grows older, it is easier to detect attachment disorders because it makes it more challenging for the child to develop future relationships. The child or adolescent may face relationship difficulties like being too attached, being afraid of rejection, or being afraid of intimacy. Someone with an attachment disorder may also be more susceptible to depression, anxiety, PTSD, borderline personality disorder, or dissociative disorders. When the child or adolescent does not have strong attached relationships in their life, it is easy to continue with emotional detachment.

PHYSICAL EFFECTS OF TRAUMA

Because toxic stress involves hormones being dispersed throughout the body and all of the body's systems being on heightened alert, trauma can have significant physical side effects that last for the short term and the long term. When the body is experiencing stress and anxiety, it can also experience a racing heartbeat, shortness of breath, dizziness, and an inability to concentrate. These symptoms might arise during a traumatic episode or when the child has a flashback from the trauma. The racing heartbeat and shortness of breath can place additional stress on the cardiovascular system, and over time that stress can deteriorate the health of the heart and lungs. Asthma is another possible side effect that can arise from damage to the cardiovascular system. The digestive system can also experience stress during the trauma or while reliving the traumatic event. Stress can cause the creation of additional gastric juices that can upset the digestive track. Many children who have experienced trauma could complain about frequent upset stomachs.

Other physical side effects may be more long term. Just as some trauma victims avoid social interaction and withdraw from society, they may also show avoidance through their physical symptoms as well. Some children will display fatigue and lethargy. The body is almost shutting down to avoid the mind thinking about or facing any additional trauma. The additional rest that the body is seeking is preventing the body from doing anything else. Fatigue and lethargy do not always mean sleep. Sometimes, the child may be tired but his brain is still thinking and worrying so much that he cannot fall asleep. Abnormal sleep patterns are very common for children who have lived through trauma.

CHILDHOOD TRAUMA LEADING TO ANXIETY

Children who grow up experiencing trauma often live in a chaotic and unsure environment. An adult may promise the child that the trauma will never happen again, but then several days later the abuse or the violence continues. Children living in trauma want relief from the trauma and are afraid of the future. Anxiety is simply deep-rooted fear. The fear becomes so predominant that it limits the child's ability to do normal activities. Trauma makes the child believe that her future will not be as good as others' future. She believes that her trauma is going to continue for years to come. Again, that creates a huge amount of anxiety.

Anxiety that is rooted in trauma is slightly different from other types of anxiety. The mental health professional can treat the anxiety, but unless the child deals with the trauma, the anxiety will return again and again. Both trauma and anxiety are treatable; however, it is essential that both conditions are addressed in the treatment plan.

Cognitive-behavioral therapy (CBT) is still one of the major treatment methods used for anxiety created by trauma. Instead of using this type of therapy to just change behavior patterns, the therapist helps the child identify issues associated with the trauma. For example, if the child is worrying about the worst-case scenario, then the therapist would work on helping the child deal with realistic challenges. If the child has nightmares about an event such as the parents' divorce, then the therapist would talk about the current reality and how to cope with the situation as it is.

One strategy for dealing with trauma is eye movement desensitization and reprocessing (EMDR) therapy. This type of therapy is newer, but it has been used successfully to decrease the symptoms of traumatic stress. During a therapy session, the therapist will ask the child or adolescent to focus on a traumatic memory. The therapists will then utilize a series of clicks, taps, tones, and directed eye movements. The child will probably be using some type of headphones to focus on the directed sounds while walking through the traumatic memory. The sounds and eye movements allow the brain to reframe the memory, possibly releasing some of the stress and anxiety from the new memory. Just like CBT, this type of therapy requires a time investment. The reduction of stress and anxiety is seen when patients attend sessions for a length of time, not an occasional drop-in session.

Another type of therapy to address trauma is prolonged exposure therapy. Patients with trauma typically want to avoid things that remind them of their trauma. Then, the more a child avoids her triggers and rearranges her life, the more the trauma begins to control the child's life. Prolonged exposure therapy allows a child to slowly begin to face her fear over time. The therapist sets up safe scenarios that relate to a feared memory or place. Then, the therapist helps the child make small steps toward conquering the fear. These steps may be very gradual. The child may initially just be able to be in the same place as the trigger, but then eventually she can work toward reducing her fears.

Some mental health professionals may also recommend alternative treatments to assist children with learning how to calm their breathing and better regulate their stress level. Meditation and yoga are both practices that help children learn how to slow down their bodies, slow down their breathing, and become more aware of their stress level. Deep breathing activities can also assist children with regulating their stress. Breathing techniques can be used in almost any setting without any props, so it is a strategy that children can learn to use when the therapist or another trusted adult is not present. Children may also be encouraged to use creative therapy methods like art or dance therapy. These strategies allow children to move and be creative to reduce their stress level.

TRAUMA PREVENTION

Although there is treatment available for trauma and the anxiety that surrounds trauma, the most consistent way to reduce trauma is to prevent it. It is impossible to prevent every traumatic event that a child could experience, but it is possible to have potential protection in place to help the home and the community be as safe and comforting as possible. For example, there are times when a parent will lose his or her job, but there are support programs in place at the local and state level to make sure that families have stable food and housing despite the loss of income. These types of supportive programs help to protect the family from trauma. Other protective factors include the following:

- Children who are part of a peer group
- Children who are doing well in school
- Children who have role models outside of their immediate family
- Families that supervise and monitor their children with rules and boundaries
- Families with a support network of extended family members and friends
- Families that have access to quality child care
- Families that have access to medical and mental health care
- Families with parents who have college degrees or higher
- Families with parents who have consistent employment
- Families that know how to work through conflict without screaming or violence
- Families that emphasize the importance of school for their children
- Families that spend time together doing fun activities

The key to helping protect families from experiencing trauma is to make sure that they have access to essential needs and have a strong support system of relationships inside and outside the family. Many families that eventually experience trauma start with a loss of basic needs or a lack of an emotional support system. Those losses lead to stress that can evolve into abuse, substance abuse, or a breakdown of the family through divorce or separation. When families are supported before stressors occur, they can use their support system to avoid further complications.

Dealing With Childhood Anxiety and Challenging Behaviors in the Classroom

II

Classroom Assessments and Professional Evaluations

9

Assessments and evaluations are an important part of the process to make sure that a child is diagnosed correctly and gets the right supports. From an education perspective, it is important to remember the teacher's role in the evaluation process and which tasks are completed by a diagnostician or a mental health professional. Classroom assessments and referrals can be completed by a teacher and can be used for the evaluation process. Formal evaluations and diagnoses are given only by licensed professionals who work specifically in the mental health field. In most cases, a general pediatrician will defer to a licensed counselor, psychologist, or psychiatrist to make the diagnosis, knowing that they are more qualified to evaluate different mental illnesses.

WHAT ARE ASSESSMENTS?

An assessment is a tool used by a classroom teacher to determine whether a child is meeting all of the developmental milestones appropriate for his age. These assessments are usually created to look at every developmental domain and analyze age-appropriate skills within each domain. There are some assessments that specifically look at one domain and only focus on the skills in that specific area.

The teacher uses the assessment tool to monitor whether the child is learning and adding skills appropriately. It also helps the teacher identify whether there are areas in which the student's growth is lagging behind. The tool can identify the specific skills with which the student is struggling, and the teacher can plan activities that help the student develop those skills.

Although many experienced early education teachers know the developmental milestones very well, they still use assessment tools to ensure that no markers are missed. This also helps to ensure that the teacher assesses every child on the same skills. The term *tool* usually means a developmental checklist that the teacher can go through one item at a time while observing the child to see whether she has the skill mastered. With some tools, the checklist may also come with materials that help the teacher determine whether the child has the skill. For example, a preschool assessment may require the teacher to have the child use a pair of scissors and try to cut paper on a series of straight or curved lines to assess the child's development of fine motor skills.

Once the teacher has completed every section of the assessment, he or she will add up the total number of points awarded for the skills completed successfully. The tool usually has a point range for students who are above typical developmental level, meeting the typical level, and below the typical developmental level. The tool usually includes a breakdown by developmental domain and possibly an assessment of the child's development as a whole.

Different types of assessment tools are used in the classroom based on the reason the teacher needs the assessment data. The most basic assessment tool is called a screening tool. A screening tool is a shortened version of a developmental assessment that lets the teacher know whether further assessment is needed. Each domain may have only four or five questions that focus on some of the major skills for that particular developmental domain. For example, the screening tool for large muscle skills for a 5-year-old may look to see whether the child can skip, gallop, balance on one foot for more than 5 seconds, and rotate feet when going up and down the stairs. If the child misses two or more of the initial items on the screening tool, then this is an indication to the teacher that a more in-depth assessment may be needed. It is standard practice in many schools to use a screening tool each year to assess children's development. Some schools use a screening tool before children enter the school (e.g., before entering kindergarten) to assess the overall development of the new students for the purpose of classroom planning.

Screening tools are often quite simple to use, and although schools may use them more than other groups, they are not the only agencies that use them. A doctor's office may use screening tools at well-child check-ups to assess a child's development. Health departments and other agencies that may assist with frontline interactions with families may also use these tools. In some states, organizations such as public libraries may also train their staff on screening tools to make sure that all families have some type of access to early intervention screenings.

Another type of assessment that is used in the classroom with young children is a curriculum-based assessment (CBA). This tool is more in-depth than a screening tool, but it does not focus on a child's development. Instead, it looks at the curriculum goals that the child should be meeting. In preschool, the CBA may look at items such as whether the child can identify shapes, colors, alphabet letters, and numbers. In elementary school, this type of tool may look at which phonics patterns the children have mastered. This tool can be used multiple times throughout the year to help the teacher identify which skills have been mastered and which skills need additional reinforcement. Typically, a CBA is created by the company that created the classroom curriculum. This way, the teacher's curriculum and the assessment tool are aligned perfectly.

Teachers are usually trained on how to use the CBA at the same time that they are trained on the corresponding curriculum. The company may work with schools and send their professional trainers to school systems when they first adopt a new curriculum; however, it is unusual for a school or preschool to pay for the brand-name training more than once. After a group of teachers has been trained initially, those teachers are often called on to train new staff members who begin teaching at the school. Many CBAs are similar, so once a teacher has been trained on how to use one, it is not a large adjustment to switch to another tool after a brief training.

Young children can also be assessed using a diagnostic assessment. This is also a tool created for use in a school setting, but the assessment may be conducted by a teacher, a special educator, or a school therapist. This type of assessment usually requires the professional who administers the tool to have in-depth training on the tool and to have received some type of certificate showing that he or she is officially trained. A diagnostic assessment is a very thorough assessment tool. Not only does it cover the developmental domains, but it usually addresses subcategories in each domain.

One of the main reasons an education professional needs a specific certification on a diagnostic tool is because the grading process can be quite complicated. The tool usually ranges over a large developmental period, and the assessor must determine when to begin asking the questions (or observing the skills) and when to stop assessing. For example, if the assessor is observing a 4-year-old child, he should not begin by observing the infant developmental milestones. The assessor needs to follow the tool's instructions for where to start and then, as the child stops showing the mastery of skills, the assessor must also determine where on the developmental spectrum to stop. Most tools call this process finding the "floor" and the "ceiling" of the child's ability range.

The diagnostic tool does give the assessor the ability to see exactly how far above or below the typical developmental range the child's skills fall. Because children all have a window of time for skills to be considered typical, it is not a problem for children who are slightly below the normal range of development. However, when a child demonstrates that she is significantly below the developmental norms, that is more concerning.

Although a diagnostic assessment gives the teacher significantly more information than the other assessment tools, it is still not a diagnostic tool. The important information that a teacher or therapist acquires from this tool includes developmental areas with which the child may be struggling as well as specific sub-areas of those domains. For example, a child may have a very difficult time with balance skills but not with all the large motor skills. Other children may show delays in all subsections of a developmental domain. For a child who may eventually be diagnosed with an anxiety disorder, she may be shown to have delays in the social and emotional domain as well as potential concerns in the language or cognitive domain. The teacher can meet with the parents to share the results of the assessment and let them know about areas of developmental concerns so that the parents can share that information with the child's doctor.

NOTICING DIFFERENCES

Although an experienced teacher may become somewhat of an expert on child development and developmental delays as she watches group after group of students move through her classroom, it is essential for teachers to remember their role in the assessment and evaluation process. A teacher's primary job is to notice differences. The teacher can observe the child every day in a group setting, and that makes it possible to obtain a large amount of information about the child. The teacher can notice the child's interests and strengths. The teacher can notice how a student behaves in a group and how he behaves independently. A teacher may also notice the situations and activities that are extremely challenging for the child, but in reality, that is where the teacher's job ends. The teacher needs to notice those differences and share that information with the family. It is never the teacher's job to diagnose.

A teacher's extensive training focuses on helping children to learn new concepts. It does not include identification and diagnosis of disabilities and medical conditions. When a teacher steps out of his specialty and attempts to diagnose a child's condition, it can have a severe impact on the child and the family. First, the teacher could make a completely incorrect diagnosis, particularly because teachers are not trained to be diagnosticians. Because the teacher is a trusted adult, the family may take the teacher's opinion as factual information and attempt to treat the child for the wrong condition. That could set the child's progress back significantly.

Another possibility is that the family could become extremely angry with the teacher for her diagnosis of the child, and their relationship may be damaged. Even if the child received the same diagnosis from a specialist, it is essential for the relationship between the teacher and the parent to remain intact. As the child begins a treatment plan, it is

so important for the teacher and the parents to work together, and we know that receiving devasting information such as the diagnosis of a mental health illness can cause the family to experience strong emotions like anger. If the diagnostician tells the family that the child has an anxiety disorder, and the family focuses their anger on the diagnostician, the family may not actually need to work with that specialist after the diagnosis is complete. The teacher will be a much more integral part of the child's support team, and the family needs to trust the teacher in order to have the best communication and cooperation possible.

When a specialist begins to formally evaluate a child, he or she may ask the teacher more questions about what he has noticed in the classroom. Often, the diagnostician may have forms for the teacher to fill out about the child's behaviors in the classroom and the developmental markers that the teacher has observed. Some of those observations are essential to complete the full evaluation process. It is also important because the teacher sees behaviors that the family does not have the opportunity to see. The teacher observes the child in a large-group setting on a regular basis, whereas the family may only see the child play alone or with siblings. In addition, the teacher observes the child having to concentrate for longer and more intense periods of time than the parents will observe at home. Some of these slight environmental differences in the parents' and teacher's observations give the diagnostician key information to help make an accurate diagnosis.

SHARING INFORMATION WITH PARENTS

When a teacher has been noticing that a child is falling behind on milestones, it is essential that she shares that information with the child's family; however, the method used to share information is just as critical as the information itself. If a teacher requests a conference with the parents, the meeting should never focus solely on negative information about the child. When the family begins the evaluation process to see whether the child has special needs, there will be so many meetings and doctor's appointments that focus on the child's deficits. The teacher needs to make sure that the parents hear the child's strengths as well as the weaknesses. Too much negative information about the child can be truly devastating for the parents.

Once the teacher has shared information about the child's strengths, the activities she enjoys in the classroom, and the children she likes to play with at school, then the teacher can begin to talk about the areas of concern. Again, the focus needs to be on what the teacher notices. The teacher notices that the child has a hard time speaking to her classmates. He notices that the child becomes worried when it is time to switch to a new part of the school day. The teacher notices that she frequently talks about having a stomachache. Once the teacher shares all the details and events that he has noticed, then the teacher can suggest that the parents talk to the pediatrician about all of these observations to see what the doctor thinks should be the next step.

WHAT IS A REFERRAL?

A referral is the formal process by which an adult in the child's life (e.g., a doctor, a teacher, a parent) requests further evaluation. In the public school system, a parent or teacher can make a referral for a special education evaluation. When it comes to medical care, the insurance companies typically require the pediatrician or family doctor to refer the child to a specialist. That specialist could be a counselor, an occupational therapist, a child psychiatrist, or a child psychologist. In some cases, these specialists will not schedule an appointment directly with the family. The appointment must be made through the pediatrician's office until the new patient has seen the specialist at least once.

The public school system, for children 3 years of age and older, has a child psychologist available for when children need an evaluation for a possible disability or mental health illness. If a parent or teacher starts the evaluation process through the public school system, then the parent will be provided with written notification that the referral was made, and consent will be required to start the special education process. When it comes to mental health illnesses, many families feel more comfortable seeking medical attention outside of the public school system and asking their doctor for guidance. Whether the referral process starts at the doctor's office or in the school building, the goal is to decide if the child needs a professional evaluation to receive more support.

WHAT DOES AN EVALUATION LOOK LIKE?

A professional evaluation of a child's mental health will typically be conducted by a licensed counselor, a child psychologist, or a child psychiatrist. Although it may sound very formal, the evaluation is usually held in the specialist's office just like a normal appointment. For a specialist who works predominantly with children, the office will most likely be inviting and have toys and materials with which a young child will enjoy playing. Prior to the actual appointment, the specialist will usually send initial paperwork to the family to fill out. These forms typically include a family medical history, but they will also include questionnaires for the family to fill out about their concerns with the child's behavior.

Once the family arrives at the specialist's office for the appointment, there is most likely going to be a portion of the assessment that will include questions for the family and a portion between the child and the specialist. Depending on the age of the child, it may be difficult during the evaluation to get the child to talk to the specialist or to answer questions. A young child may not want to speak during his first visit to the office. If there are toys and materials in the room, that may provide one way for the specialist to observe the child's behavior. Also, if the parent is in the room with the child, that may present an opportunity for the specialist to observe the interactions between the child and the parent.

To determine a diagnosis, the specialist will use a multimethod approach when interacting with the child and the family. She may start off by trying to interview the child and the parents. The child's interview will be based on his or her level of comfort with speaking to someone new. The parent questionnaires, filled out in advance, will be a key part of the diagnostic process. There may also be additional forms for the parents to fill out once the specialist obtains some background on the child and has more information on what type of mental health illness the child may have. Because the teacher is a daily observer of the child, the specialist may also ask the parent to give the teacher questionnaires about the child's behaviors in the classrooms. These types of forms usually list a wide variety of mental health behaviors, and the parent or teacher records whether the behaviors are present. Some types of questionnaires may address the frequency and severity of the behaviors. Finally, the specialist will be observing the child during the observation. It is not unusual for the evaluation visit to be much longer than a typical visit so that the specialist can observe the child's behavior long enough to answer important questions on the screening tools. Although different specialists may prefer different name brands of questionnaires and screening tools, the process remains the same.

WHAT DO EVALUATION RESULTS MEAN?

The results of the evaluation are determined once all the questionnaires, rating scales, and observations have been reviewed. The specialist will then give the family a diagnosis. That official diagnosis is the condition on which the treatment plan will be based. If a child psychologist or child psychiatrist performed the evaluation, then he or she may only see the child every few months once the treatment plan is started. A counselor is the person most likely to see the child for therapy on a regular basis. A child psychiatrist will still see the child, but their visits are likely to be less frequent. Any appointments with the child psychiatrist are more likely to focus on monitoring medication if that is part of the treatment. Child psychiatrists are often in high demand for evaluation and medication monitoring, so many of them do not have room in their schedules to see children on a weekly or biweekly basis for cognitive-behavioral therapy or play-based therapy. A child psychologist is also usually consulted for evaluation purposes.

Although regular therapy will allow for a counselor to assess a child's progress, both insurance companies and the public school systems require intermittent reevaluations to see whether the child's condition remains as severe as at the time of diagnosis. If the child has made significant progress since the time of diagnosis, then she may no longer need regular therapy. Of course, if a child is diagnosed with a chronic mental health condition, there may be times when it is better controlled than others. A child may have a period when therapy is not required; however, triggers and changes later in life may require the child or adolescent to seek therapy again. In the public school system, a reevaluation is needed for an individualized education program (IEP). Insurance companies may vary on how they proceed. If the child has a concrete diagnosis from previous years, a new referral and evaluation process may not be required in order to seek treatment again. Other insurance companies may require a reevaluation to see whether the child's need qualifies her for treatment and how many treatment sessions the company will approve.

Comorbidities With Anxiety   10

A comorbidity is when a child has more than one condition at a time. Comorbidity means that the conditions are co-occurring. A comorbidity is not a health complication from an illness or a medication. A side effect is a condition that develops during one disease due to its treatment or due to how the progression of the illness affects the rest of the body. A comorbidity is a separate condition occurring to the same child at the same time.

A comorbidity can dramatically affect a treatment plan for a child. If the child has two or more illnesses that must be treated, then the illnesses can have different triggers and different symptoms. That means that the treatment plan may basically be doubled if the conditions' treatments do not align with one another. Often, comorbid illnesses do have similarities, so the child may see the same type of specialists (e.g., counselors, occupational therapists, psychiatrist) to treat all present conditions.

Although comorbid illnesses do not create one another, there are illnesses that are more likely to occur in the same individual. For example, when it comes to medical conditions, diabetes, obesity, and heart disease are often comorbid conditions. Obesity does not create heart disease, but there is similar stress on the body when all of these conditions are present. For mental health conditions, it is likely that the child or adolescent could have more than one anxiety disorder at a time, or it is possible that a child with anxiety could have a comorbidity of depression. There are other childhood diagnoses that have a comorbidity of anxiety. Often, if a diagnosis has a component of social and emotional developmental delays, then it is also likely to have a comorbidity of anxiety. Some children with chronic medical conditions, such as childhood cancer or cystic fibrosis, have a comorbidity of anxiety due to the emotional strain that the medical illness exerts on the child.

A doctor treating a child with comorbid conditions not only needs to think about multiple treatment plans, but she also needs to think about how multiple medications can affect the child. When a child must take multiple medications to treat one or more conditions, it is called polypharmacy. Of course, a doctor tries to not prescribe medication for a child if it is not necessary, but if more than one illness requires medication, it can become complicated. Medication can work well for a child when it is the only medication that is taken; however, two medications taken together have the potential to cause more harm than good if their formulas do not complement one another. It is possible that a child consistently takes one medication for a chronic health condition but then that child needs to take medication for a common illness. If the child's family does not communicate to the general practitioner about what medication he routinely takes, then even the onset of a simple illness can cause complications when additional medications are added to the child's routine.

A key factor in treating comorbidities is to make sure that every specialist and medical professional working with a child has a full family and medical background. Once this information is in the practitioner's computer system, the system is likely to flag any contradictory treatments or medications that cannot be taken together. Family history can also be essential regarding comorbidities because it tells the specialists about illnesses with which the child has a higher percentage chance of being diagnosed at some point in time. If a child has a family history of epilepsy, then the practitioner is less likely to prescribe a medication with a possible side effect of seizures. All of this past medical information can help a child avoid any unwanted health complications.

CHILDHOOD DEPRESSION

One common comorbidity for children with anxiety is depression. The National Alliance on Mental Illness (NAMI) stated that 60% of children with anxiety also have depression (NAMI, 2018). Childhood depression is marked by significant sadness that is persistent and affects the child's daily routines. Symptoms of depression can vary from child to child, but overall, the symptoms are marked by hopelessness, persistent sadness, and mood changes. Other symptoms include the following:

- Anger
- Social withdrawal or isolation

- Fatigue
- Changes in sleep routine (sleeplessness or continuously sleepy)
- Changes in appetite
- Feeling worthless
- Feeling guilty
- Crying or screaming
- Inability to focus
- Physical symptoms such as stomachaches and headaches
- Sensitivity to rejection
- Loss of interest in school, poor academic performance

Causes of childhood depression, just as in adults, can be due to a wide variety of reasons. Children may be predisposed to depression if there is a strong family history. A child's physical health, life events, and environment can all have an impact on depression. Depression is not just a temporary bad mood, and it will require treatment to improve. If a child's persistent sadness lasts a minimum of 2 weeks or longer, then it may be time for a parent to contact the pediatrician about the child's symptoms.

The evaluation process for depression is very similar to the evaluation process for childhood anxiety. There will be interviews for the parents and the child, as well as behavior questionnaires for parents and teachers. The mental health specialist will also want to get a family and medical history and observe the child's behavior. Treatment will most likely include counseling or medication. The most successful treatment usually includes a combination of both. Many medications used to treat childhood depression can have significant side effects, so it is very important for the medication process to be closely monitored by a medical specialist.

AUTISM

Autism is a developmental disorder that includes social, communication, and behavioral delays, and it is now prevalent in as many as 1 out of every 44 children (CDC, 2022b). When a child is diagnosed with autism, a common comorbidity is childhood anxiety. NAMI (2018) showed that 40% of children with autism have a comorbidity of anxiety. Most children with autism begin to show signs of the disability before the age of 3, even though the diagnosis might not come until later. Symptoms of autism include the following:

- Avoiding eye contact with others
- Preferring to play alone rather than with others
- Having trouble interpreting other people's feelings
- Having trouble expressing his or her own feelings
- Being sensitive to touch, preferring not to be held
- Avoiding playing pretend games

- Repeating the same actions
- Being focused on one particular obsession
- Using self-stimulatory behavior (e.g., hand flapping, spinning)
- Having trouble adapting to changes in routines
- Having strong sensory reactions to sounds, smells, tastes, and touch
- Repeating or echoing similar words or phrases
- Not understanding sarcasm or jokes
- Not knowing how to initiate interactions with others

Children can be diagnosed with autism as young as 18 months, but many children are much older when a diagnosis is finalized. Unlike with some disabilities, there is not a specific medical test that can detect autism. A child psychologist typically performs the assessment for autism, and the most common testing instrument is called the Autism Diagnostic Observation Schedule–Second Edition (ADOS-2; Lord et al., 2012).

When the child psychologist is evaluating the child for an autism spectrum disorder diagnosis, there are several specific traits that must be present:

1. Limited social-emotional responsiveness, social-emotional attention, or social exchanges;
2. Deficits in nonverbal communication; and
3. Difficulties with peer interactions (ZERO TO THREE, 2016).

Because children with an autism diagnosis struggle so much with social interactions, it is easy to see why they may also experience anxiety such as social phobia. Any type of social interaction can be very overwhelming depending on how much intervention the child has had.

There are no known causes for autism. However, organizations such as the Centers for Disease Control and Prevention (CDC) have documented trends that have been noticed in children who have been diagnosed with autism (CDC, 2022b):

- Children who have a sibling with autism have a higher rate of autism diagnosis.
- Children who were born to older parents are more at risk for an autism diagnosis.
- Children with certain genetic conditions, such as fragile X syndrome or tuberous sclerosis, are more at risk for an autism diagnosis.
- Children who were exposed to certain prescription drugs during pregnancy, such as valproic acid and thalidomide, are more at risk for an autism diagnosis.
- There is some evidence that the critical period for developing autism happens before, during, and immediately after birth.
- Autism occurs in every economic and social group, but it is four times more likely in boys than it is in girls.

There many different treatment approaches to autism. Those approaches include behavioral, developmental, educational, social, and psychological therapies. Behavioral therapies include applied behavior analysis (ABA) therapy. ABA therapy encourages positive behaviors and discourages negative behaviors. Therapists break down lessons into very simple steps and reward all positive behaviors in the lessons. Developmental therapies include speech, physical, and occupational therapy. The speech therapist may focus more on the process of communicating with others than on the words and vocabulary that the child needs to use. The occupational therapist may focus on self-help skills and sensory integration skills.

The social-relationship model focuses on using social stories to help children know what to expect in social situations and to help them practice social situations before interacting with same-age peers. The psychological approach will use cognitive-behavioral therapy (CBT) to help the child learn new behaviors that they can use in social situations and that follow social rules. During CBT, the therapist and the child will establish goals that they will work toward together.

Children with autism can also receive a lot of support in the public school system. A child with autism can receive an individualized education program (IEP) in the public school system with special education services to help the child be as successful as possible. Those support services can include speech therapy, occupational therapy, social-emotional services, and time with the general special education teacher. Although the child may have no cognitive or academic deficits, the social and emotional delays can cause the child to show poor academic performance due to defiance, failure to talk or interact with others in the classroom, difficulty with transitions, or social anxiety.

ATTENTION-DEFICIT/HYPERACTIVITY DISORDER

Attention-deficit/hyperactivity disorder, commonly known as ADHD, is a childhood neurodevelopmental disorder. It is a lifelong diagnosis of a disorder that often causes children to have a difficult time concentrating, poor impulsive control skills, and high levels of energy (CDC, 2022b). The National Alliance for Mental Illness (2022a) showed that 25% of children with ADHD have a comorbidity of anxiety. The full list of symptoms for ADHD includes the following:

- Forgetting things often
- Tending to daydream
- Being extremely talkative
- Fidgeting constantly
- Making frequent mistakes
- Taking unnecessary risks
- Having a hard time taking turns with others or waiting for others
- Exhibiting aggressive behaviors

There are two different types of ADHD, one type that presents with inattention and the other type that presents with impulsive and hyperactive behaviors. A child may also show signs of both types where she is inattentive at times and overly active at other times. Just because a child presents as predominantly inattentive when she is younger does not mean that the presentation will not change over time. The same child could show impulsive and hyperactive tendencies in later adolescence or as an adult. The presentation can change over time.

The risk factors and causes of ADHD are variable just as with other diagnoses such as anxiety disorder and autism. The CDC does list several potential factors including genetic factors, low birth weight, premature birth, possible brain injury, prenatal exposure to drugs or alcohol, or environmental factors such as lead exposure (CDC, 2022b). The public has speculated that too much screen time or increased levels of sugar are contributing factors to ADHD, but there is no research to support these suggestions.

The diagnostic process is slightly different for the inattentive type of ADHD compared to the hyperactive and impulsive type of ADHD. According to the *Diagnostic and Statistical Manual of Mental Disorders, Fifth Edition (DSM-5)*, diagnosticians look for five to six characteristics present for at least 6 months (APA, 2013). When diagnosing inattentive ADHD, the diagnostic criteria include the following:

- Failing to pay close attention to details, or making careless mistakes in school
- Trouble holding attention on tasks
- Appearing not to listen when someone is speaking to him or her directly
- Failing to follow through on directions
- Difficulty organizing tasks
- Refusing to do tasks that require focus for a long period of time
- Frequently losing items necessary for tasks
- Displaying distractibility

When diagnosing impulsive and hyperactive ADHD, the diagnostic criteria include the following:

- Constantly fidgeting with hands and feet or squirming in seat
- Constantly leaving seat when the situation requires him to sit down
- Running and climbing indoors when it is inappropriate for the situation
- Inability to participate quietly in activities
- Being always on the move
- Talking incessantly
- Displaying impulsivity (e.g., responding before a question is complete)
- Having difficulty taking turns

The diagnostician also looks to see if these traits are present in more than one setting, if the traits were present before the age of 12, and if the traits can be explained by another diagnosis.

The treatment plan for ADHD typically includes a combination of behavioral therapy and medication. The parents may also be encouraged to receive parenting classes to support and discipline their child in the most appropriate ways. Children younger than age 5 are rarely diagnosed with ADHD. It is usually diagnosed in early elementary school, but in very extreme cases there may be a diagnosis at the preschool age. Treatment for ADHD may include medication more often than in other diagnoses at this age range.

Many parents and doctors also consider the child's overall health when putting together a treatment plan. They look at the child's nutrition and attempt to increase fruits and vegetables while decreasing added sugar. They look at helping children participate in regular, if not daily, physical activity and they also look at setting limits on computer and screen time. Finally, many parents also monitor the child's average nightly sleep to make sure that their body is getting all the necessary rest.

MOOD DISORDERS

Another comorbidity with childhood anxiety is childhood mood disorders. Aside from childhood depression, this category also includes bipolar disorder and disruptive mood dysregulation disorder (NAMI, 2018). Bipolar disorder includes extended periods of highly elevated moods followed by a time of low or flat affect. Disruptive mood dysregulation disorder is characterized by complete inability to control and regulate the body's emotions. The causes of mood disorders are not well understood. There is a belief that genetic factors or brain chemistry could play a large part in these disorders. There could also be environmental factors, such as chronic stress, that contribute to mood disorders. Symptoms of a general mood disorder include the following:

- Sadness, depression, irritability, or anger
- Periods of elevated moods
- Difficulty interacting with family
- Changes in sleep patterns, eating patterns, or weight
- Physical symptoms including stomachaches, headaches, or fatigue

- Lack of motivation to participate in normal activities
- Poor performance in school
- Reoccurring meltdowns or anger outbursts
- Rebellious or high-risk behaviors
- Feelings of shame, guilt, or low self-esteem
- Running away or threats of running away
- Difficulty interacting with peers

A licensed counselor or a child psychiatrist is often the specialist who diagnoses a mood disorder. At the time of evaluation, the specialist may request a full medical history and family medical history, a list of the child's symptoms, a list of the symptoms in the home compared to school, input from teachers and school counselors, a list of potential emotional stressors that could be affecting the child, and a history of the child's past experience with therapy and medication (NAMI, 2018). A treatment plan for a child with a mood disorder may include individual therapy (most likely CBT), family therapy, and medication. Consistency of the treatment is a key part of the treatment plan. A child with a mood disorder may need regular therapy for months or even years. Short bursts of inconsistent treatment may only complicate the condition. Families and children will both need to dedicate time to improving the child's mental health.

DUAL DIAGNOSIS

There are other impacts that a comorbidity or a dual diagnosis can have on the family. The financial strain may increase due to additional therapies and medications. Sometimes, the same specialists can treat the child for both conditions, but one condition may need supports that the other condition does not require. It can also impact a family to make arrangements to transport a child to multiple types of therapy each week. Additional family members or friends of the family may need to be involved in the child's treatment so that the parents can work and the child can still get to all required appointments.

There is also a greater strain on the other members of the family once the child has additional medical and mental health needs to consider. At some point, the parents completely forget about their own needs to take care of the child; however, that can often lead to more than one member of the family dealing with increased mental health needs. It is essential for the family members to remember their own needs from time to time to make sure that the family continues to function as a healthy unit.

Partnering With Parents   11

When parents first find out that they are going to have a new baby, they instantly start to dream. They have huge dreams for their baby. They dream about the decorations for the nursery and the clothes they will buy. They dream about what kind of person their child will become. Will the child be kind, funny, independent, or dramatic? They dream about what school their child will go to and what job their child will have one day. They dream about ballet classes and football practices. Most parents dream about family traditions, such as spending Christmas morning with their children or the family vacations they will take together. Once they finally get to hold their baby in their arms for the first time, they then have a face to see in those dreams and they want the best for their child from that point forward. Parents want to offer their child the world, and they want better for their child than they ever had for themselves.

When a young child is diagnosed with a special need, whether it is a disability or a mental health disorder, it can cause those dreams to feel unattainable. Parents had expectations of what their child's life was going to be like, but the diagnosis may prevent some of those expectations from ever happening. A child with significant anxiety may never stand on a stage during a ballet recital or perform in a school musical. A child with social anxiety may not have the large group of friends that the parents anticipated for him. Instead, he may feel safer at home, and a parent may feel like he is missing key childhood experiences. A child with selective mutism may not get good grades in school if a teacher cannot hear her read out loud and grade her progress. These types of changes to parents' dreams can be devastating. Of course, parents will go out of their way to love and support their children, but they also must deal with the loss of the child that they expected to raise.

CHRONIC SORROW

Chronic sorrow is the mourning that a family goes through when they are faced with the reality that the perfect life they planned for their child is not going to occur. The family must mourn the loss of the child they planned on, even as they begin to support the child that they have. This process does not mean that the family does not love their child. It does not mean that the family would choose a different child if they had the chance. It simply means they are experiencing a loss, and there is great sadness attached to that loss. Just like typical grief, chronic sorrow is recurring and overwhelming at times. It will reemerge for parents at different times in the child's life when parents see other children meeting milestones that their child may never accomplish.

This type of profound sadness often occurs for the families of children with disabilities, chronic health conditions, and mental illnesses. It is normal for the mind and the emotions to go through this period of grieving, and it is normal for the grieving to resurface at points when the parents thought they had already worked through their grief. Overall, it is an internal battle for the family to accept *what is* compared to what they thought *should be*.

It is important for the family to remember that although they will experience periods of great sadness, they will still experience contentment and joy during their child's life. With disabilities and mental health diagnoses, the child will experience periods of progress but there will also be setbacks, and family members will also have setbacks when it comes to their grief. This is a typical progression. Symptoms of chronic sorrow include feelings of loss, guilt, exhaustion, burnout from caregiving, and comparing a child to their typically developing peers, as well as anger, bargaining, and other stages of grief.

STAGES OF GRIEF

Chronic sorrow is the process of the family grieving over the life their child could have had in a perfect world. Because that sorrow is based in grief, it is important for families to understand the process of grief and the emotions that will accompany that grief. When someone experiences a significant loss (such as the death of a loved one or, in this case, the loss of their dreams for their child's life), they will progress through the following stages of grief:

1. Denial and isolation
2. Anger

3. Bargaining
4. Depression
5. Acceptance

Denial

The first stage of grief is denial. When a parent enters this stage of grief over a child's mental health, he or she usually denies that there is anything wrong. The parent may be adamant that the child is only going through a phase, but he or she will not admit that the child has a permanent condition or diagnosis. The parents may be approached by family members with concerns about the child, and they may refuse to hear their concerns. The teacher may voice concerns in a parent–teacher conference, and the parents may immediately end the conversation or become defensive that the teacher even broached the topic. If the parents willingly discuss their concerns with the family pediatrician, they may ask for reevaluations or a second opinion from another specialist.

If the family is experiencing this level of denial, then they may begin to isolate themselves from their friends and family members because they do not want to discuss the topic. They don't want anyone else to show them indisputable facts and try to prove them wrong. The parents may even isolate themselves from the child to some degree in order to avoid seeing the behaviors that are glaringly obvious. The more time they spend with their child or with other children the same age, the more likely they are to see the differences in their own child. So, instead of acknowledging these differences, they attempt to be alone or spend too much time at work to deny the obvious.

If the parents finally get to a point where they are willing to look at the information and be rational, they still may have moments where they think, "this can't really be happening, not to me or my family!" The specialists, the teachers, or even a close friend may have to wait for the parents to process some intense emotions before they are ready to hear the information again at a time when they may be willing to accept it.

Anger

The second phase of grief is anger. This stage occurs once the family finally accepts that there is a problem and the child needs help. At that point, the family is typically looking for someone to blame. They may blame a teacher for having a stressful classroom, or they may blame a doctor for not providing what they consider to be appropriate care to the child. With a mental health condition, the parents may blame a family member who has a history of mental illness and be angry at that person for passing down the condition. Parents may even be mad at themselves or at the other parent for creating a situation where the child feels anxious. Ultimately, the family is angry and they desperately want to be mad at someone in particular.

When there is not a specific person to blame, the family may just be mad at everyone they encounter. They may be mad at their faith or their god for not protecting their child from the situation. Regardless of the target of the anger, most parents spend time being angry but will eventually realize that the anger is not helping them or their child. At that point, they move on to the next stage of grief. It is important to note that many people can get stuck in this stage of grief and stay angry for quite some time. That may be the point when the parents need to seek counseling of their own to deal with the sorrow and grief that they are experiencing.

Bargaining

The third stage of grief is bargaining. At this point, the parents may be trying to make a deal with the universe or with God to heal the child or solve the problem. Most parents try to bargain by pleading to go through the experience themselves if their child can be spared. Others may beg for their child's healing if they promise to "be good" for the rest of their lives. They admit that the child's condition is real, but they are looking for any possible miracle that could take the diagnosis away. Once the parents continue to offer one deal after another with no obvious miracle, then they are at a point where sorrow has increased and depression takes over.

Depression

Depression is the fourth stage of grief. In the context of chronic sorrow, depression is expressed in two different ways. In the first way, the family is sad and constantly worried about the child. The parents may focus on how sad the situation is for hours on end, but at the same time, they get up every day and do what they need to do to support their child. The second type of depression is much more profound. It may be subtle to detect, but the family slowly begins to give up. The parents have stopped fighting for the family and the child to live a normal life. They simply exist, and they do not work to battle the condition. Some parents may have looked for their own mental health supports earlier in the grief process, but if they have not yet obtained counseling, it is critical to do so at this point. This type of depression will slowly seep into every part of a person's life and begin to harm the entire family. Parents have many options for support. They may utilize a support group for parents of children with special needs or mental health needs, regular clinic counseling, or counseling from a religious leader. The key point is that the parent must receive support and come to realize that the situation is not as hopeless as it may seem.

Acceptance

The fifth and final stage of grief is acceptance. Acceptance only comes after experiencing a rollercoaster of emotions, and some people will never achieve this step in the process of grief because they become stuck in anger or depression. It is also possible for someone to achieve acceptance but have a setback and revert to an earlier stage of grief. Grief can be a cyclical and fluid process that changes as the child's condition changes and as outside factors affect the parents' emotional stability. One key point in the process of grief, whether the family is lodged in anger or acceptance, is that the parents must find daily ways to cope with their child's condition and their own mental health. That may mean that each parent needs to find ways to include self-care in their own routine (e.g., exercise, counseling, time alone) so that each can be healthy physically and emotionally. When the parent is healthy (physically and emotionally), he or she is going to be more likely to offer better care to the child.

MENTAL HEALTH STIGMA

Although many families must learn to care for a child with special needs, there are still some stigmas attached to caring for a young child with a mental health condition. Many people appear to be understanding of a family raising a child with a disability or a chronic health condition, even though those diagnoses were also somewhat taboo at one time. There is still a great deal of misunderstanding when it comes to a young child diagnosed with anxiety or depression.

Friends or acquaintances may blame the family for creating an environment where the child is anxious. The parents may be embarrassed to tell others that their young child experiences anxiety or needs to see a therapist. Many people have strong negative feelings about putting a young child on medication for any reason. Of course, it is never the first choice of any family to give their child medication. However, those who are not close to the family may not know how much the child's diagnosis is preventing the entire family from living a normal life. In those cases, the parents must make the best possible decision for the child and family, and sometimes that decision includes medication.

During the COVID-19 pandemic, many families became aware of the mental health needs of young children. They noticed how isolation, disrupted routines, and fear of an unknown illness created significant burdens on the mental health of young children. Some of these realizations have started to change the general population's perspective on starting treatment for proper mental health at a young age. This new perspective could be one positive by-product of the pandemic. As communities learn more about the impact of anxiety on young children, it may be easier for families to tell their personal stories to friends and neighbors. Until all families feel comfortable sharing this information, it is critical for them to remember that their child's treatment plan is not up for debate in a public forum. The individuals who do not know their child, or their child's situation, do not have the right to weigh in on whether the family is handling things correctly. Ultimately, the family must make the best decision for their child, and in the end, that is all that matters.

PARENTING CHILDREN WITH SPECIAL NEEDS

It is difficult to be a parent regardless of the circumstances. There is no manual that tells an adult exactly how to parent their child "correctly," and other individuals offer a myriad of opinions—whether or not the parent asks for help. With that said, parenting a child with

special needs is even more challenging. The parent can stay constantly overwhelmed, exhausted, and confused. Along with all of the characteristics of grief, parents of children with special needs also have many other traits in common.

Exhaustion

Being a caregiver is always an exhausting role, and when a parent is caring for someone who has very demanding needs, it can cause tremendous physical, emotional, and mental strain. Consider attending therapy, going to doctor's appointments, giving medication, and attending school support meetings, and the parent may feel like it is a full-time job just to meet the needs of one child. When you add in work at or outside the home, marriage, caring for other children, and household duties, it feels like more than one person can possibly bear.

Isolation

It is extremely easy for the parent of a child with special needs to become or even feel isolated. Not only will the time required to care for the child prevent the parent from participating in normal activities with friends and family, but the parent can feel alone simply because others do not understand the burden of taking care of a child with such complicated needs. Friends may encourage a parent to get a babysitter and come out to socialize with them, but they don't understand what that involves. A child with special needs cannot have just any babysitter. The child needs someone who understands the condition, who can help with medication or treatments, and with whom the child is connected enough to feel safe while the parent is gone. Even simple activities, such as a night out with friends, can be quite complicated, and the parent may not have anyone else who understands.

Jealousy

A parent whose child has special needs may be unintentionally jealous of friends who have children who are typically developing. They may not be jealous of the child, but they may be jealous of the experiences that their friend is having with their child. They may be jealous that their friend has more free time, the ability to leave their child alone in the backyard for a short amount of time, or the opportunity to take a vacation without their child. Parents may feel guilty about feeling jealous, but it is a normal emotion and part of the grieving process for parents who experience these differences.

Fear

Many parents of children with special needs have a plethora of fears. The fears will vary based on the significance of the child's needs, but overall, they are afraid of what their child might not be able to have or do, or of what the future holds. Will my child be able to live alone one day? Will she be okay when I die? Will I be able to pay for all her medical bills? Will we find the right treatment? Am I doing everything I can to help her? All of these fears lead to the parent fixating on the worst-case scenario. Ultimately, everyone has fears, and they are unavoidable. The key is for the parents to focus on what they can do to help their child and what small wins they experience each day.

Protective

All parents want to protect their children, and that desire is even greater when a parent feels that the child is vulnerable in some way. People who are uneducated about a child's special needs may make rude remarks like calling a child "crazy." These types of comments feel like slander or accusations. In most cases, it is someone who simply does not know how his or her words can make another person feel. At the same time, a parent wants to make sure that the child knows all the wonderful characteristics they display, instead of the shortcomings. Calmly letting someone know that their words have a negative meaning can make a world of difference to some people. In other cases, the parent must learn to ignore the comments that come from the uneducated and disrespectful few.

Imperfect

This can be so hard for a parent to admit, but unfortunately, all parents make mistakes. It seems so much more devastating when that parent is making decisions for a child that impact his or her ability to have a normal life. Parents will try to make the best possible decisions. They will educate themselves on their child's condition, and they will learn about all of the recommended treatments. They will learn about medications and all of the possible side effects. They will learn what type of supports the school can offer and how the school can help their child. They will do their research and decide what they believe will benefit their child. At times, these decisions will be wrong. The parent will need to accept that he or she is not perfect, and then try to move on to the next best decision. The sting of a mistake can be painful, but there are usually so many more successes than failures.

ADVOCATING FOR THE CHILD

Parents become advocates for their children long before a diagnosis is made. As soon as a parent notices that something seems different or wrong with the child's development, it is important for the parent to begin speaking up. Sometimes, a doctor may not see the difference immediately. A doctor may see the child for a 15-minute appointment, but the parent is with the child day in and day out. He or she is the expert on that child, and that expertise needs to be considered by all doctors, teachers, and specialists the family talks to about developmental concerns.

If the doctor or teacher does not want to make an initial referral, the parent can begin to document all the situations that have occurred that are concerning, or they can seek a second opinion from another professional. Some agencies will let the parent make the referral and then the agency will perform an evaluation based solely on the parent's concerns. Insurance companies may dispute what services they can pay for, such as evaluations, continuing therapy, or annual visits. Parents must learn the skilled art of battling with insurance companies and overwhelming them with documentation explaining why a child needs a certain service or medication. It is always possible to change the insurance company's decision, but the parent must be persistent.

Parents may also need to advocate for their children in their school setting. Although a child may have a mental health diagnosis, the school may not believe that the diagnosis affects the child in their education setting. The parents need to make sure that they know the parent rights for special education in their state. They need to document all the ways that the child's condition can impact him or her in the classroom setting and how that will affect the child's education progress in the long term. A parent can request a school evaluation and begin the process for assistance. A mental health diagnosis may not require an individualized education program (IEP) in the public school system where the child receives additional services, but the child may qualify for a 504 plan, which the school needs to make accommodations for the child's condition, such as additional time on tests due to test anxiety.

The key to advocating is not how knowledgeable the parent is but how willing he is to fight for his child. Of course, it is beneficial for a parent to know the child's condition and all the characteristics that come along with that condition. At the same time, that parent can still demand a referral from a doctor or an evaluation from the school without having concrete evidence. The parent is always the expert on his child, and he is the best person to stand up for the child no matter the circumstances.

Stephanie's Story

Robbie was 7 years old when he was diagnosed with generalized anxiety disorder, and at the time I was stunned. I had seen how aggressive he had been, and I saw his defiance. I did not think that meant an anxiety disorder. After all the screaming, hitting, and temper tantrums, I finally made an appointment to take him to a counselor. I thought he had some sort of behavior disorder. I also wondered if we had just spoiled him and created the situation ourselves because he was our youngest child. I set up the initial appointment with the counselor, and she told me to come to the session ready to explain my concerns. I had a list of the behaviors I was worried about, and I was ready to share them with her as soon as we arrived at her office.

During that first session, I was in tears talking about how difficult our home life had been for the past 6 or 7 months. Robbie's temper tantrums lasted for so long, and they did not make sense to me. He was so much more upset than the situation ever warranted. When he would really get overwhelmed, he would start screaming and eventually start hitting me. He never became aggressive at school, only at home. I was usually the target of his aggression, but he would occasionally hit and kick his big brother. I had bruises all over my arms and legs because I tried to stop him hitting me without hurting him in the process. His tantrums would occur in public places such as the store or our church, and people I had never met before would come up and offer me parenting advice or tell me that their mother would never allow them to behave that way when they were his age. All that ever did was make me feel ashamed. We also had instances when Robbie would run away from us completely. We were at a baseball tournament for his older brother when he ran away from us, and it took 12 others to track him down. As I told her all the details, I realized how disrupted our family life had been for months.

At the end of our session, the counselor told me that she did not think that Robbie had a behavior disorder. After observing him and talking with me, she said that she felt confident saying that he had an anxiety disorder, and she believed that his anxiety level was very significant. She began talking to me about how to move forward with treatment. She wanted us to see a child psychiatrist to get her thoughts as well, but she also thought that Robbie's anxiety was significant enough that we may want to consider giving him medication to reduce his anxiety and help him be more successful during the day. It took a while to find a child psychiatrist who could take Robbie on her caseload. I also found out that many of the child psychiatrists in our area do not accept insurance. They only take cash. I had wonderful health insurance that I paid a lot for, but it wasn't going to help us this time. The cost was big, but more than anything, I wanted to help my son.

I brought the same list of concerns with me to the child psychiatrist, and she also agreed with the counselor that Robbie had generalized anxiety disorder. She said that she gave him this diagnosis because his anxiety seemed to affect all areas of his life, and his anxiety seemed very disproportionate to the actual situations he was worrying about each day. She did mention that his social anxiety seemed to be a large trigger for his meltdowns. We also talked about how strong his fight-or-flight reactions were when he became anxious. That really helped me understand all the aggression I had seen. When he was anxious, he would physically fight me to get away from the situation, and if that didn't work, he would run away. As I talked more with the doctor and the counselor, Robbie's past behaviors began to make sense, but I never would have identified them without help.

As we learned more about Robbie's diagnosis, we began to develop his treatment plan. Robbie saw the counselor once a week. Because he was still very young, we chose to take him to a play-based therapist. She worked with him on trying to identify his emotions and how to calm down when he became very upset. Robbie also went to see an occupational therapist once a week. She also worked with him on learning to calm down his body, but she focused a lot on his social anxiety and helping him feel more successful in social settings. My husband and I did choose to put Robbie on an antianxiety medication. We weren't sure at first whether that was the direction we wanted to take, but when we saw how much of his day he spent worrying, we needed to help him find some relief. We saw the child psychiatrist every 3–6 months so that she could monitor how Robbie was doing on his medication and see whether it was still the best course of treatment.

Finding the right treatment plan for Robbie lifted a huge weight off our family, but he is still living with a mental health diagnosis that affects our whole family every day. When the diagnosis process first started, I thought that Robbie was only experiencing anxiety over events or situations that he dreaded. That is not the case. He can be looking forward to something, such as a sleepover at his grandfather's house, and still experience increased anxiety for days beforehand. Sometimes, he worries about complex issues, things that a 7-year-old should not have to worry about, and that causes his stress.

We have had to make a lot of changes to our everyday life. We don't watch the news or listen to podcasts with world news so that Robbie doesn't begin to worry about national or global issues. We try to have very structured routines at our home so that Robbie isn't worried about what happens next. That doesn't always work out. One day, I picked him up after school and told him that we had to run an errand. He began to cry and started asking so many questions. "Where is it? How long does it take to get there? Will we be home before dinner?" Just listening to his list of questions made me realize how much the unknown affects him.

Although we have always communicated with his school a lot, Robbie's treatment plan made that communication even more important. As soon as we received his diagnosis, I went to the school guidance counselor to set up a 504 plan so that the school could make accommodations in the classroom for his anxiety level. The school administration does things such as tell us early who his teacher is for the new school year, and they let him come to visit his new classroom over the summer so that he won't worry about his classroom change. His teacher and I both let the other know if one of us must travel or change our normal schedule so that we can prepare Robbie for those changes.

Although the school has done everything possible to help, there are days when they call and my heart breaks. I have received a phone call from the principal telling me that Robbie had a meltdown and tried to run away from school. The staff did not let him leave, of course, but it always scares me a little when I hear stories like this. Robbie now wears a GPS clip on his clothing that is made for children with special needs. I have an app on my cell phone that alerts me if he tries to leave the school grounds. These are measures that I never thought I would have to take as a parent, but now I am willing to do anything to keep my son safe.

Social settings are still really challenging for us. Meeting new people always makes Robbie anxious, and adults often get frustrated with him when he won't speak to them after an introduction. New buildings with lots of new faces can make him very anxious, so we may have to drive by and see the building in advance if we know that we have an event coming up.

Then, there are days when things are just "off." As with any chronic illness, there are some days that are better than others. On challenging days, there may still be screaming and hitting during a large meltdown. I understand now that the meltdown occurs when Robbie is so overwhelmed that he can't process all the emotions he is feeling. It is not a manipulative temper tantrum like I once thought it was. That doesn't mean that it is easier to deal with just because I understand it. Some days are truly exhausting. I feel a level of fatigue that I almost can't express, and it is physical as well as emotional. I want to have the energy to be the best mother possible, but it doesn't always feel that way when your son is lying on the floor kicking and screaming without being able to tell you why.

Sometimes, I think it is harder to tell people that my child experiences anxiety than if he had a condition like Down syndrome or cancer. When someone says that their child has Down syndrome, everyone seems immediately empathetic. When I tell someone that my child has an anxiety disorder, they get this look on their face that says, "What did you do to him to make him so stressed?" Honestly, sometimes I wonder that myself. Did I do this to him? He has never witnessed abuse, domestic violence, or drug or alcohol abuse. He has lived in the same house since he was born, with his biological parents and his brother. We have never worried about where we would live or how to afford our next meal. He goes to a wonderful school, and our family is very involved. Even with all that in his favor, he still has significant anxiety, and at times it just doesn't seem like it should have happened to us.

Those worries lead to guilt and more stress. The stress is abundant. I worry about what his life will be like after high school. Will he still have all the normal experiences, such as college, dating, marriage, and parenting? Those are wonderful experiences, but they are still very stressful. By that time in his life, will he have learned the coping skills that he needs to be successful and enjoy those opportunities?

I also worry about the stress that this puts on my older son. He is as patient as he can possibly be, but he lives with a difficult little brother. Unfortunately, that difficult brother gets extra attention, and I don't want my other son to feel forgotten or neglected.

There is also my full-time job to worry about, my health, and my marriage. These all take time and energy, and on some days, being a special needs mom has taken all the energy I have. Things like going back to school after a week of spring break are normal events for most families. At our house, recovering from a week without a routine and going back to school can be stressful for a week or two to follow.

I worry about the money that it takes for medication, two therapy sessions a week, and occasional visits to the child psychiatrist that cost several hundred dollars each. Most people rarely use their health insurance, but we meet our annual deductible in February each year. I also worry that Robbie is now old enough that his friends can notice he has to go to all these appointments. They see the teacher making accommodations for him at school. For a child who struggles with social anxiety, when will it start to worry him that his friends realize he is slightly different? He must take his medication to church camp and sleepovers. He can't play with his buddies after school because he is with the counselor. Eventually, these differences are going to catch up to us, but right now, those differences are the supports that keep us going each day.

While I am doing all this worrying, I also see an amazing little boy. I see Robbie's creativity and his boundless energy. I see his gentle side when he is relaxed, and I wish the whole world could see that side of him. I see his sense of humor and how he makes everyone in our family laugh. I see his amazing memory. On most days, his memory is working against him because it makes him remember everything that he can worry about, but I see how he remembers details of conversations from years ago or fun days with our family that he will never forget. I wish that one day, those are the characteristics the world will see first, because there is so much more to Robbie than his diagnosis.

Classroom Interventions 12

It is essential for a teacher to understand the students' needs in the classroom, but once the teacher knows the special needs of all the students, that information must be used to make the classroom a nurturing learning environment. This can mean that the teacher not only needs to modify the classroom teaching style but also the physical classroom environment. Classroom modifications may be easier in the preschool classroom than in the elementary school classroom due to the academic demands of elementary school. Despite the more rigid learning environment, it is important to remember that if a child's essential needs are not met (e.g., a feeling of safety while at school), then he will not progress to higher levels of learning. Classroom interventions must be taken seriously, and they will be more successful with the collaboration of the child's parents and the special education team.

CREATING ROUTINES

Routines are repeated, predictable events that are an established part of a child's daily tasks. Routines can be for the entire classroom or they can be individualized to meet the needs of each child. A child's morning routine may include saying goodbye to his father, hanging his coat up, going to his desk, and beginning his morning work routine. Another child may have a slightly different morning routine when she arrives at school early to go to the cafeteria to get breakfast and then proceed to the classroom. A child's routines should match her level of independence so that she can be as successful as possible on her own. The routine also must match her skills for self-regulation. The most challenging part of the routine for most children may be separating from the parent, so the routine needs to be predictable for the child and set up in a way that makes her feel comfortable. So, despite how tired the child is or what the parent has on his mind, the sequence of the routine needs to stay the same for the child as often as possible.

In the preschool classroom, the daily activities may include drop-off, circle time, free play, outside time, restroom time, circle time, lunchtime, naptime, restroom time, free play, outside time, and dismissal. Because the free play period may be anywhere from 1 to 2 hours, the preschool schedule can be simpler than an elementary school schedule that may have 30-minute increments for its activities. That schedule may look more like this: arrival, morning work, whole-class reading, small-group reading, table work, special activities, lunchtime, whole-class math, table work, social studies or science activities, outdoor playtime, and dismissal. These portions of time are the schedule, not the routine. It is also important to have a consistent schedule so that children with anxiety understand what to expect next. The times of the scheduled activities are not as important to the children as they are to the teacher. The child is more worried about the order of events so that he can predict what comes next. The child may also focus on activities such as a special class that changes each day. He may consistently ask which special class is occurring so that he can prepare his expectations.

Outside of the schedule, a child may have many other important routines embedded in the classroom. It can be very overwhelming for an elementary school–age child to enter a large cafeteria, so to cope with the experience, she may create routines to guide her through it. For example, her routine may include getting in the same line each day, selecting chocolate milk, looking for the same food service worker to give her a meal, reciting her lunch account number at the register, and going to her seat. If the routine is a coping mechanism for the child, then it can be distressing when she must skip a step in the routine. For example, if her preferred lunch line is closed or if the cafeteria is out of chocolate milk, then her anxiety level can instantly increase. This may cause her to struggle with the rest of the routine, such as remembering her lunch account number at the register.

A child who is dependent on routines can learn to cope with changes to the routine, but it is often best when he has time to prepare for the change. One large change to a routine would be having a substitute teacher in class. This can be very stressful for the child because he does not know what to expect from the new teacher. *Will she change the class routine? Will she be kind? Will she like me? Will she let me go to the bathroom if I ask her?* All of these variables can easily cause anxiety to increase.

One way for a child to prepare for this type of change is for the teacher to prepare the child in advance. On a completely normal day at the beginning of the school year, the teacher can explain to the child, or to the whole class, what will happen if she must be gone from school one day. She can empower the children to have helping jobs in her absence and assist the substitute teacher. She can explain that the assistant teacher will still be there. Another way to prepare for this type of change, if possible, is for the teacher to contact the family and let them know that she will be absent so they can prepare the child for the change. It can also be very helpful for the family to do the same thing if a family member has a dramatic change, such as the mother traveling for a day or longer. This way, the teacher can prepare for that change in routine in the same manner.

These predictable routines can be so important for young children. They establish safety. They help the child to stay at ease and self-soothe. When the child feels safe, it allows her to focus on her academic learning instead of only worrying about whether she is safe. When a young child feels at ease, he is more able to talk about his needs, so he feels more capable of open communication with the teacher. The consistent routines also allow a child to develop stronger social skills with peers and less familiar adults. When the child can move through the motions of a routine safely, she has the concentration and bravery to interact with others. When the routine is unpredictable, a child with anxiety may be using all her concentration and bravery to focus on the next step of the routine. The consistency takes away part of that additional stress.

CALMING STRATEGIES

A child diagnosed with an anxiety disorder will have times when he is so overwhelmed that he cannot regulate his own behavior. When this happens in the classroom setting, it is important for the teacher to have a tool kit of techniques to help the child calm down. Although children can have a wide variety of triggers for an anxiety attack, once the attack has begun, the primary focus is on helping the child to calm down and begin to self-regulate

once again. Determining the trigger can happen later. Once the anxiety attack has begun, the child may not be rational enough to describe what made him upset or why it is illogical to be upset at that moment. The only focus should be on helping him resolve the anxiety to a comfortable level. Here is a list of techniques to assist a child with calming down:

1. Blowing bubbles: Blowing bubbles requires a child to focus on breathing. Instead of blowing as many small bubbles as possible, it will benefit the child to blow one large bubble, which will require deeper breathing.

2. Give the child a weighted vest or a weighted blanket to wear for a deep-pressure feeling. If the teacher chooses to use a deep-pressure item, such as a blanket or vest, it is essential that the vest or blanket be made for the size of the children in the classroom. If the blanket or vest is too heavy, it can make it difficult for the child to take deep breaths.

3. Have the child wear noise-resistant headphones to block out all other classroom sounds.

4. Provide the child with a bag of fidget or sensory toys to play with until he can self-regulate.

5. Provide a yoga mat and yoga picture cards in one corner of the classroom that children can use when they want to slow down their bodies.

6. Offer the child a movement break outside of the classroom where an adult can allow the child to run, crab walk, or bear crawl or to perform other deep-pressure movements.

7. Cooked spaghetti: Have the child lie down on the floor and first pretend to be uncooked spaghetti, where she makes her entire body tense to look like a straight line. Then, tell the child to be cooked spaghetti and wiggle around on the floor. Ask the child to go back and forth from these two movements from a tense position to a loose position.

8. Body-part squeeze: Have the child stand up and tell him to focus on squeezing his toes as tightly as possible. Count to 5 and then release. Squeeze one more time and then release. Move up the body, isolating individual body parts from the toes to the top of the head to create a focus on tension and then release.

9. Deep belly breathing: Have the child lie on the floor. Take a small toy, such as a miniature car or a small stuffed animal, and place it on his stomach. Ask the child to take deep belly breaths and watch the toy go on a roller coaster ride. The goal is for slow breaths that show the child that the stomach is moving up and down. When the car or the stuffed animal fall off the stomach, then the child gets a point. See how many points he can collect while doing deep breathing.

10. Make a burrito: Use a regular blanket from the classroom's calm-down area and wrap the child tightly like a burrito for a deep-pressure feeling.

11. Provide the child with play dough or therapy putty to use.

12. Use a "calm-down jar": Calm-down jars are an easy craft in the preschool or elementary school classroom. The teacher can use an empty water bottle and fill it with water, cooking oil, and glitter. Make sure to secure the top of the jar with something sturdy, such as strong glue. The child can shake the bottle aggressively and then watch the glitter slowly float around the bottle. It has the slow and calming effect of watching a lava lamp or fish swim in a fish tank.

13. Blow on a pinwheel: Teachers can keep a couple of pinwheels in the classroom just to help children who need to focus on breathing. This can have the same effect as blowing bubbles but without the mess. The teacher can prompt the child to use one slow breath or short bursts of air. The overall purpose is to focus the child on her breathing patterns and eventually begin to self-regulate again.

14. Become an artist: When some children become anxious or angry, art supplies can be one of the best cures. A lot of classroom "calm-down" corners include a bag of art supplies to use to draw or color. It may also allow an upset child to tell the teacher about what triggered his anxiety.

15. Bubble wrap: Having extra bubble wrap in the classroom can be a great way to help a child self-regulate. Due to the sound of the bubble wrap popping, this may be an activity to do in the hallway or outside. Allow the child to jump up and down on the bubble wrap to take out any frustration or anxiety. Once the child begins to slow down (or becomes tired), she may be able to express her emotions with words again.

16. Tennis-ball rolling: The teacher can use a tennis ball for extra sensory experiences in the classroom. Have the child stand up and lean against a classroom wall. Put the tennis ball between the wall and the child's back. The child leans on the tennis ball, rolling the ball on the wall without letting it fall and hit the ground. The activity creates deep pressure and allows the child to focus on the game of not dropping the ball.

Several of these activities require some practice for the children to be able to complete the activity at a heightened stress level. This means that a child needs to practice the activity when she is not anxious or stressed so that she is able to complete it when she is anxious. Many of these activities would be appropriate to practice with the class as a whole, such as the entire classroom practicing yoga poses together on a day when they cannot go outside for recess. Other activities might be something that the child could practice during free play or that the special education teacher could practice with the child.

Depending on the support services that the child receives at school and through private therapy, a young child may be able to tell the teacher exactly what she needs to do when she feels panicked. Depending on how much the child relies on consistent routines, she may want to use the same tools each time she needs to calm down. In that case, it is very easy to keep certain tools available for her.

In elementary school, a child may be increasingly anxious about having to read in front of peers or participate in group projects. The teacher can help reduce the child's anxiety level by doing things such as the following:

- Letting the child know a day in advance what chapters or passages the children will need to read out loud in class the next day. An anxious child then has the opportunity to go home and practice those sections before having to read in front of peers.

- Having students read out loud in small groups instead of reading in front of the entire class.

- Preparing the child in advance to participate in a group project and letting him have some control over who is in his group or what his job responsibility in the group will be.

- Using computerized reading programs where the children can independently read a passage on the computer and then answer comprehension questions. This is an alternative that can be used occasionally instead of always reading out loud in class.

CREATING SAFE SPACES

When children become anxious in the classroom, particularly children with social anxiety, they often want to go to a private place to calm down. Of course, a classroom with 20 children does not usually have a private area, so many teachers have started to create a "calm-down" corner in their classroom where children can be alone. This area should not be a part of the dramatic play area or a section of the classroom that is overly visible to others. This area is not a disciplinary tool to be used for time out. A child would choose to go to the calm-down area, as opposed to being forced to be there.

This would be a separate area that is only big enough for one child at a time. Most likely, the students would need an introduction to the calm-down area with some guidelines on how to use it. This area may be a tent, a teepee, a large cardboard box, or any type of small structure that gives the child some level of privacy as she begins to calm down and self-regulate. The calm-down corner would also have some type of toolkit to help children calm themselves down while they are there. Many calm-down corners provide materials such as art supplies, bubbles, a blanket, fidget toys, or stuffed animals to squeeze. The supply kit should be based on the needs of the children who use it.

Another aspect of creating safe spaces is for children to understand the classroom rules and the consequences of breaking those rules. This can specifically apply to the way that children interact with each other. If there is one child (or more) in the class who is likely to be unkind or aggressive to the other children, then the other children are going to feel safer if consistent classroom rules are established and there is follow-through for those rules.

Children often feel more invested in classroom rules when they get to help create them. Sitting down with the entire classroom of students at the beginning of the year to talk about how children treat one another can be a great way to start off a safe classroom climate. Even very young children can articulate that it is not right to hit, kick, or take materials away from the other children. If the children create rules and are guided to create reasonable consequences, then they will feel like they have more control over the classroom climate.

Regardless of who creates the rules, there will always be times when a child breaks those rules. In those cases, it is imperative that the teacher has consistent follow-through. The other children are less likely to feel safe in a classroom environment where the teacher gives one child seven or eight reminders not to hit but never allows that child to experience a consequence. Consequences do not have to be harsh. A natural consequence is often the best follow-through for very young children. A natural consequence is a consequence that would happen in natural circumstances and is directly related to the action that occurred. For example, if a child throws a block, then the natural consequence could be losing her privilege to play in the block area for a designated period of time. This would not be a permanent punishment, but only a temporary consequence to show her how her actions can impact her classroom privileges.

It is not a natural consequence to take away a child's outside playtime every time he breaks a classroom rule. The playground is rarely related to the actions that occur inside the classroom. Also, the children who have more elevated behaviors inside the classroom are often the children who need to run and play on the playground to regulate their level of energy. Unstructured outside playtime is something that almost all children value, so it can easily be turned into a motivational factor for children to behave indoors; however, if the teacher threatens to take away playground time, then he needs to follow through on that consequence when the child breaks the classroom rules. That consequence is likely to backfire on the teacher when the child has pent-up energy later in the school day from not having had the opportunity to run on the playground. It works out so much better to directly connect consequences with the action that was taken. Instead of creating a huge consequence, it is better to have small consequences that follow immediately after one reminder. Having consistent boundaries can be a comfort for young children because they know exactly where the limits are and how far they can go.

ZONES OF REGULATION

The Zones of Regulation is a technique created by Leah Kuypers, an occupational therapist who often worked with children who had a difficult time controlling their bodies (Kuypers, 2011). She based her technique on four different colors that represent different emotions children might be experiencing. If some young children have a challenging time expressing the emotions they are feeling, they could potentially identify a color and the variety of emotions represented by that color. Green represents a calm state of alertness, and it includes emotions such as happy, proud, calm, and focused. Yellow represents a heightened state of alertness with emotions beginning to rise. Yellow includes emotions such as worried and frustrated, or silly and excited. Red represents intense emotions with a high state of alertness. The red zone includes emotions related to being angry, panicked, terrified, or overjoyed. The final color is blue, which represents a lowered state of alertness. It includes emotions such as sad, sick, tired, or even bored.

The zones are often compared to traffic signals. The idea is that the child learns to identify the emotions associated with each color and can then communicate which color zone she is in. Once the child can identify her zone, then she can also begin to brainstorm how to move back to the green zone or how to prevent moving from the yellow zone to the red zone. The program has several benefits for young children, such as using consistent language that helps them to learn how to identify their emotions without constantly being introduced to new vocabulary. Another benefit is that the concepts are relatively simple, and they can easily be used at home, at school, and in recreational settings. Teachers can implement the program throughout their classrooms because it is very inclusive and works for children with and without special needs.

Some children may need to use pictures of people's faces to initially identify the emotions linked to each color. This will be particularly critical for children who have a hard time identifying other people's facial expressions and emotions. The teacher may ask the child to make faces that match what he looks like when he is sad, angry, apprehensive, or happy and take pictures of his expressions. The teacher can take those pictures and place them on the associated color background to help the child with color recognition.

INCREDIBLE 5-POINT SCALE

The Incredible 5-Point Scale (Buron & Curtis, 2021) is another program developed to help children learn to identify their emotions. The program, created by Kari Dunn Buron and Mitzi Curtis, also focuses on identifying emotions, but it relies predominantly on a number scale instead of strictly using color identification. The number scale also allows the child to identify the intensity of emotions. Number 1 of the Scale focuses on a happy, content demeanor, and number 5 is an intense or elevated emotion. The Scale can be adapted to focus on tone of voice (e.g., no talking, whispering, classroom voice, outside voice, screaming), emotions (e.g., happy, anxious, frustrated, overwhelmed, angry), or other areas such as body space or anxiety level. The Incredible 5-Point Scale is also used by therapists and special educators, but it is a tool that can be used in a classroom with children who are typically developing. It may be used with slightly older children than the Zones of Regulation because the vocabulary can be expanded and different concepts can be explored with the Scale.

The Incredible 5-Point Scale can be a huge asset to students with social and emotional delays and students with mental health diagnoses because many of these students are visual learners. This Scale takes content that is objective and makes it more concrete by looking at the differences in facial expressions. It is very beneficial for a student to see that a meltdown does not occur in one dramatic step. Watching the escalated steps of intense emotions can show children exactly what is happening when they begin to get more upset, and it can show them that at any point they can choose to move back to the step below.

ACCOMMODATIONS FOR SOCIAL ANXIETY

The early childhood classroom is set up for children to wander and explore, but many of the activities in the classroom can still cause a great deal of social anxiety. Teachers may not even be aware of the stress that the classroom environment has established. When the teacher is making accommodations for children struggling with social anxiety, the goal is not to eliminate activities altogether from the classroom, but instead the teacher can find a way that the child may choose not to participate in activities that can cause additional stress. The heartbreaking part of this discussion for many teachers is that some of the events that the teacher and many of the students look forward to each day, or each year, may be the very activities that create a great deal of anxiety for others. Some of these activities include the following:

- Singing welcome songs at circle time
- Having a calendar helper during circle time
- Having a student of the week
- Having birthday celebrations
- Having special dress-up days
- Having a family member come to class as a guest reader or volunteer
- Having classroom performances

A student who experiences social anxiety does not want to receive social attention whether that attention is positive or negative, so even classroom events that celebrate the student can make the student very anxious. Some social experiences focus on celebrating one child, and that can be extremely stressful for a child with anxiety, but the same child can still be anxious when it is a special day for every child in the classroom. For example, if the classroom plans a pajama day or a crazy sock day, all the children in the classroom will be invited to participate in the event. From an outside perspective, one particular child is not going to be singled out. However, the children are excited to see what all their classmates will wear on these days, so they will go around and inspect everyone's costume. A child with anxiety may have each one of his classmates come up to him and evaluate what he wore to school that day, and that much attention can be overwhelming.

Even the stress of a routine activity can be overwhelming when every person in the classroom focuses their attention on a child struggling with anxiety. For example, when the students arrive at school in the morning, many teachers begin the school day with a circle time to greet all the students, take attendance, and give instructions for morning activities. A normal part of that circle time may be singing some type of hello song. If the hello song identifies each child individually, then that can again turn the entire room's attention to the child who does not want to be noticed. A teacher does not need to stop singing hello songs or stop having circle time, but she may need to change the way that she implements them. For example, when she sings the hello song, she may ask students to raise their hands if they want her to sing a greeting to them, or she could make the hello song part of the pick-up routine when the children are putting away toys and joining one another on the rug. That way, an anxious child may not choose to join the circle time until the hello song is over.

Events that single out one specific child can be a little more complicated. If every child in the classroom has a birthday celebration, then the teacher may need to ask the child with social anxiety if she also wants to have a celebration for her birthday. She may want to bring a treat to school to share with her classmates, but she may not want all the children to look at her and sing "Happy Birthday." That is a perfectly reasonable accommodation. If the children ask why they are not singing, it is fine for the teacher to say that their friend does not want them to sing. Some teachers may feel like the student is missing out on some of the best childhood experiences by passing on these types of events; however, it is important to remember that a child is not having happy childhood memories if she is hiding under the table because of anxiety as her classmates sing "Happy Birthday" to her.

The teacher may need to make additional accommodations for classroom performances to determine how involved an anxious child may want to be. Some children may willingly participate in a music performance or a classroom play even if they are nervous, but others may need significant accommodations. Those adaptations can range from a smaller child standing in the back so that the audience cannot see him to an extreme where he may learn the music with his class but ask to not stand on the stage during the performance. The younger the child is, the more accommodating the teacher should be. Although one day the child may need public-speaking skills, he does not have to develop them in preschool or even elementary school. Not everyone wants to be a performer, and if the experience is so stressful that the child never wants to participate in this type of activity again, then it was not a learning experience for the child.

Since the onset of the COVID-19 pandemic, virtual learning has become more common. Very young children have mastered the art of logging on to a virtual meeting to learn a lesson from their teacher in a remote setting. Unfortunately, virtual learning has created its own spin on social anxiety. When a young child logs on to a videoconferencing meeting, the first thing she sees is a screen full of people who appear to be looking back at her. For a child with social anxiety who may not prefer to make direct eye contact, this can be extremely overwhelming. Of course, each virtual learning platform has some method of changing the view so that the child may see fewer participants. Despite those changes, the screen can trick the child into thinking that multiple people are looking her in the eye at one time.

Depending on the age of the child, different accommodations can be made. Preschool-age children may prefer to place a stuffed animal in front of their camera and then sit off to the side of the computer screen where the faces are not visible. If the teacher changes the screen for everyone to look at a book or a slide deck, then the child may feel comfortable sitting closer to the screen. Older children may just move to the side of the computer where they can hear the discussion but avoid viewing the faces. Children always have the option to turn off their own cameras as an accommodation, but it is not their own camera that can be so overwhelming; it is all the other faces that can be hard for the child to adjust to seeing.

It is not necessary for the teacher to eliminate every social situation to help the child be successful. That may be more of a hinderance in the long term. The goal is for the child not to be forced into social situations that can be made easier for the child with some simple adjustments. Mandatory participation in circle time for a preschool child is not necessary. Most children still hear and absorb the content of circle time if they are quietly playing in another portion of the room. A teacher may worry that the child is not learning the classroom routine or is not learning new material if he is not at the circle with the rest of the children; however, if the child is at circle time and experiencing strong anxiety symptoms, he is not listening to what the teacher is saying—he is only trying to survive an uncomfortable moment. The accommodations need to be made to create the most nurturing learning environment possible.

Strategies to Avoid   13

When a teacher is considering how to support a child with anxiety in the classroom, it is important for him to remember that the main goal is not to completely eliminate the child's anxiety. Instead, the classroom should be set up in a way to help the child learn to manage her anxiety. With that goal in mind, there are several strategies that a teacher should keep in mind to help the child be as successful as possible.

UNREALISTIC EXPECTATIONS

The teacher should not set unrealistic expectations for the student. The student views the teacher as an expert, so if the teacher tells the student that she should not be anxious at all, then that is what the child feels is the realistic expectation. When she can't meet the expectation, then she could be emotionally devastated and even more anxious about facing her fears next time. In all reality, both children and adults feel fear regardless of whether they have a diagnosis of anxiety. Children need to be aware that it is okay to experience fear, but they don't want fear to stop them from living their daily lives. Acknowledging a child's emotions is essential. The teacher should tell her that he understands that she is afraid and that's okay. At the same time, the teacher does not want to encourage the fear. If the child tells him that she is afraid of going to the doctor, he does not need to respond by explaining all the reasons the child should be afraid of going to the doctor. The main role of the teacher and other supportive adults is to listen and support the child through the fear.

EXCESSIVE REASSURANCE

It may seem that anxious children need a large amount of praise to take on large challenges, but likely, excessive praise can be damaging to children with anxiety. For children who already tend to be anxious, excessive praise seems to set the standard very high for their future performances, so they become worried that they will not be able to maintain that level of performance in the future, further increasing the stress level. Anxious children already fear failure. If they believe the praise that they did an exceptional job once, then they usually believe it is less likely that they will be able to duplicate that level of success in the future.

This does not mean that a teacher should not offer any praise. Encouragement and praise for a success is crucial. Some of the most beneficial compliments for young children include explaining the details of what the adult saw them do (so the child will know that the adult was paying attention) and then congratulating the child on his success. The praise should be appropriate to the amount of the challenge for the child and how much hard work the child put into the task. It is very important for the adult to avoid descriptions like "perfect" that make the child believe it would be hard to duplicate the action again.

CREATING UNNECESSARY ANTICIPATION

Preparing a child with anxiety for a change in routine can be challenging. It is important to give him a small warning so that he can adjust to the upcoming changes and prepare his mind for the new situation. It is not helpful to create unnecessary stress and anticipation by telling him about an event weeks and months in advance. For example, if the parents know that they will be taking a trip in 2 months, telling the child 2 months in advance and letting him focus on that anxiety can create a heightened stress level. Instead, it may be better to let the child know a week in advance that the parents will be leaving town and his grandfather will be coming to stay with him.

Sometimes, it is impossible to wait until closer to the date of an event to let the child know that a big event is coming, like the birth of a new baby. In that case, the parents will need to be prepared for an increased stress level and reassure the child throughout the pregnancy. The parents may need to collect additional resources to help the child manage his stress, like reading books about being a big brother or making sure that the child has been around other babies so that he will know what his new brother or sister will look and sound like. The slow progression of a pregnancy often brings events that help the child work through concern about the milestones of preparing for a sibling, such as getting the new baby's nursery ready.

Although some events might be impossible to hide, it is necessary for the teacher and the child's family to determine how much stress the child can handle and to wait until closer to the date to make sure that early information does not cause unnecessary stress.

SHOWING FRUSTRATION

Supporting a child with significant anxiety can be an exhausting process. Caregivers often experience a level of exhaustion that is hard to explain to someone who is not responsible for caring for another life. When a teacher or a parent is burnt out from constantly caring for others, it is easy to become frustrated by even the smallest meltdown that a child has. Despite the frustration, it is essential to remain calm whenever you are supporting the child through a meltdown so that your emotions do not increase their stress level.

During the height of a meltdown, the child is completely illogical. She is not in control of her emotions or her body. Once she has calmed down from the meltdown, she may be able to reflect on what has just happened, and the frustration level of her teacher or parents will be one of the things at the front of her mind. Many children with anxiety already experience low self-esteem and deal with feelings of worthlessness. When they realize the emotional toll they are taking on the people whom they love and trust the most, it can cause them to feel even worse about themselves. Many children will instantly begin apologizing once their meltdown is complete, or they may begin telling their caregivers how much they love them as a slightly different attempt to say, "I'm sorry." When the adult remains calm during the child's heightened anxiety, it allows the focus to remain on the child once the panic resolves. The adult can help the child to feel safe again instead of the child worrying about whether the adult is upset.

ALLOWING A CHILD TO HIDE FROM FEARS

When a child begins to avoid her fears, she creates a distance between herself and her fear. The more distance there is between the child and her fear, the harder it is for the child to get a realistic picture of what that fear is like. For example, Isabel is afraid of the speech therapist who comes into the classroom each day to work with some of the other students. She was initially startled by the therapist one day when she heard his very low voice, and she is already apprehensive of adults she does not know. After Isabel saw and heard the man for the first time, she began to hide from him each time he entered the classroom. She did not see the other children who seemed very happy when they spent time playing word games with him during his classroom visits. Instead, Isabel would run to the back corner of the classroom and hide in the dramatic play area behind the clothes until he left the room.

At first, the teacher thought it was funny that she hid from the speech therapist when he entered the room, and she showed Isabel how to hide behind the play clothes so that no one would see her. The behavior has gone on so long that Isabel is truly scared of a man whom the rest of the children in the classroom adore. Since she has stayed removed from him, she only envisions him as a threat and has not realized that there is no reason to be afraid. The teacher initially helped her avoid her fear (thinking it would not evolve too much), but now the fear has escalated.

When parents and teachers purposefully go out of their way to shield children from their fears, the fear usually continues to grow. Whether it is a parent who delays a child's vaccines because he is afraid of needles, or a teacher who always lets a child eat lunch in the classroom because he is afraid of the cafeteria, the child's fear will not stop by avoiding the fear. At the same time, the teacher or the parents should not purposely expose the children to additional fears that can cause an extra layer of stress. The most appropriate path is for the family and the teacher to support the child through the fears that they are faced with on a normal basis without trying to add or subtract from those normal encounters.

USING BELITTLING LANGUAGE

Although an adult may see how insignificant a child's fears truly are, the fears are not insignificant to the child. Most likely, they were not insignificant to the adult when he or she was young, but with age, the adults in the child's life have naturally learned perspective. Although the child may be disproportionately reacting to his fears, it is still important to acknowledge that he is anxious and that his anxiety is negatively influencing his behavior. Some of the following statements may have good intentions behind them, but they can make a young child experiencing anxiety feel belittled or even mocked:

- It's not a big deal.
- Just don't worry about it.
- There's nothing to be afraid of.
- You're imagining that.
- If you're afraid to do it, I will.
- You just need to get some sleep and you'll be fine.
- You are overreacting.
- Stop thinking about it.

Regardless of whether the fear is real or imagined, it is important to acknowledge that the child is afraid and that you are there to support him no matter what.

OFFERING MEDICAL ADVICE TO THE FAMILY

Many people have strong feelings about how young children should receive medical treatment. Some individuals do not believe in giving children medication for behavioral or mental health diagnoses. Other families believe that alternative, natural therapies are more appropriate than prescription medication. Regardless of the teacher's philosophy on medication, the teacher needs to support the family's choice and respect how the parents choose to support the child. In fact, if the teacher is truly supporting the family, the parents and the child should never be able to discern the teacher's opinion regarding their medication choices.

Problems tend to arise when the teacher voluntarily offers his opinion or when a parent asks the teacher's opinion and he states that he would never give his child medication. The truth is that the teacher is not a medical professional, and he has never had to live through the situation that the family was in before the child was medicated. Without that knowledge and experience, he is not able to offer an educated opinion on the child's needs. The best answer from a teacher when a parent asks if they are making the right decision is for the teacher to state that he is there to support the family with whatever decision that the parents feel is in the best interest of the whole family.

Most teachers would not tell the parents that they disagree with the family's choice, but it is important to remember that offhand comments made during the school day can also affect the entire family. If a teacher makes a small comment to a colleague about too many children taking medication or if he asks the child leading questions about how the medication makes her feel, not only can those comments make their way back to the parents, but they can also make the child concerned with the parents' choices. It can be very challenging to get a young child to take medication on a regular basis. Some children have a strong gag reflex, and it is hard to swallow. Some children may hide their medication in their cheek and spit it out later because they don't like the taste or the way it feels when they swallow. It can take some time to get a child in the normal routine of taking medication, but if they think a trusted adult, such as a teacher, does not approve of them taking medication, then they begin to question whether they need it.

Most teachers would never purposely make a comment to a young child about whether he should take his medication. It is those throwaway comments said to a friend that a child may accidentally hear that can have a harmful effect, and children hear far more than they are supposed to hear. One of the complicated aspects of medication for mental health conditions is that most of it needs to be taken consistently to have the desired effects. Sporadically taking the medication will not help the child, and in some cases, it can have a negative effect on the child's health. If a child begins to doubt whether he should take his medication or if the medication has any benefits, then he may not take it consistently. This is when it could lose effectiveness or cause complications. Because it is necessary for the medication to become a routine part of the child's life to receive the best possible effects, it is necessary for all members of the treatment plan to support the parents' decisions and work together to support the child as best as possible.

LACK OF COLLABORATION WITH FAMILY

Aside from the child's medication routine, there are many other ways that the teacher needs to collaborate with the parents to make sure that the child is successful in school and in other settings. Some families make it so easy to collaborate because they seek out the teacher.

The parents bring in updates from the doctors and specialists, and they make sure that the teacher is aware of any small change to the child's routine. They request parent–teacher conferences, and they ask for the small accommodations in the child's special education plan. They initiate all the conversations, so it is very little work on the teacher's behalf.

Other families are more challenging to communicate with on a regular basis. It is obvious that child development and special education are not in their skill set. When the teacher asks the parents their opinion on how to deal with the child's behaviors, the parents just defer back to the teacher and tell her to make the decision. After a while, the teacher often begins to make those decisions without the parents because they are not offering input. It is easier to cut out one step when in the end the teacher knows that she will make the final decision anyway.

What is essential for the teacher to remember is that even though the parents don't know the terms for the special education plan, they do know their child. They know what his favorite book is, and they know what TV show he likes to watch on the weekend. They know that his favorite meal is fish sticks with tater tots, and they know that he loves mint chocolate chip ice cream for dessert. The parents know that their son's favorite place on Earth is his grandfather's house because he can swim in the backyard pool. They know that he snuggles with his dog when he gets upset and that his bedroom walls are covered with pictures that he has drawn himself. Those types of facts are priceless when it comes to developing an education plan that motivates a child. The parents might not even know how valuable that type of information is until someone sits down and tells them. That type of information can help the teacher create her classroom "calm-down corner." Those facts can be part of the conversation that redirects a child when he is emotional and needs to refocus again. Those facts can be part of the conversation that helps him learn how to interact with his peers.

Parents are also extremely important when it comes to implementing an emotional behavior system across settings, like the Zones of Regulation (Kuypers, 2011) or the Incredible 5-Point Scale (Buron & Curtis, 2021). The teacher needs to take the time to explain the system to the family and coach them through potential sticky situations. Once the parents understand the system, then it can be used at home and school. That strongly enforces its effectiveness and allows the child to understand the same set of boundaries across settings.

Many families are apprehensive to participate in setting up a child's education interventions because they do not feel like experts on education. If the teacher and special education team can explain to the parents that they only need to be an expert on the child, then they may be much more interested in joining the planning process. Of course, there are always families who feel too busy to participate, and the teacher must go after them and press them to be a part of essential meetings. This can be extremely discouraging for the teacher, but it is important for him to remember that this collaboration will ultimately help his student, and that is the highest goal.

ONLY BEING CONCERNED WITH THE SCHOOL DAY

The purpose of the public school education system is to support children whose disability interferes with the learning process. There may be some children with a diagnosed disability or mental health diagnosis that does not seem to impede their academic learning. In those situations, the school district may say that the child does not need a special education plan because the child is able to achieve good grades despite the diagnosed condition. In those cases, the teacher needs to take a step back from the school system policy and look to see how the whole child is developing, not just the academic scores. For example, Lily was diagnosed with generalized anxiety disorder. Two years ago, she was having meltdowns in the classroom every day, but she has made a lot of progress. During the day, she can stay focused on her work, and she has been able to make a few friends in her classroom this year.

The teacher reached out to Lily's mother to brag about all of her progress, and Lily's mother was stunned. She said that this year has been the most challenging that they have experienced. From the moment Lily is picked up from school, she is overly emotional and is very physical with her family members. They cannot get her to sit down and do her one-page homework on most days, and some days she is too emotional to even eat dinner. Lily sees a counselor after school 1 day a week, and the counselor has suggested that Lily is working so hard to follow the rules at school and do her work there that she has no focus and control left by the time her mother picks her up from school. The counselor has created a list of strategies that could be used during the day at school to give Lily some breaks from concentrating, but the teacher is worried that any changes to the routine could cause Lily's behavior to regress.

Lily's mother reached out to the guidance counselor at her elementary school to talk about strategies to help Lily even out her behaviors over the day instead of having such opposite behaviors in the two different settings. The guidance counselor responded by reiterating that Lily's behavior at school has been fantastic, and she told the mother that it sounded like her evening behaviors were a "home problem, not a school problem." The question to ask at this point, as the school and the parents are trying to support an elementary school–age child, is whether there is a difference between a "home problem" and a "school problem."

Eventually, the difficulties at home will affect the school day. First, if the child is refusing to do her homework, then that affects the school day, but there are emotional consequences for the school day as well. Disrupted sleep patterns and skipped meals can only occur for so long before they begin to affect the child's academic performance. The heightened stress level at home will eventually affect the school day as well. It is far too complicated for a young child to compartmentalize stress so that she is only showing anxiety in one location.

There is also an ethical dilemma for the teacher in this situation. If the practices used in the school day are negatively impacting the child's home life and routine, then is the school really doing what is best for the child? It is wonderful that Lily is showing progress at school, but if the school progress is done with the direct result of regression at home, then the teacher needs to consider that the child's needs are not being met and the school is contributing directly to that.

Teachers need to be challenged to think about the whole development of the child instead of looking solely at the academic development. Partnering with the family in regular communication can make it obvious when the child's development begins to suffer in one setting. There are times when a child may struggle with certain settings, such as going to a loud sporting event surrounded by strangers. Entering an unusual environment with an overstimulated sensory system can be overwhelming for anyone, especially a child who struggles with changes in routine and social situations. The difficulties in that environment would have nothing to do with the progress in the school setting. However, the home environment should be one of the more consistent settings that the child is exposed to each day, and if the school setting progresses at the cost of the home environment, then the education plan for the classroom setting needs to be reevaluated. Academic learning is crucial to a young child's success, but it is not the only important thing in a child's life. In fact, if a child's emotional health and security is not well taken care of, then the child will have a difficult time continuing to advance in an academic setting. Teachers have the crucial role of helping the child to grow and learn across settings, to see them continue to develop across domains. It is important for the elementary school teacher to see grades as one part of the child's development but also to remember that social and emotional skills are crucial for the child throughout her lifetime. Even when the school system is focused on academic progress, it is important for the teacher to speak on behalf of the child and remember that development in each of the domains is essential for the child to be as successful as possible.

Conclusion: Charlie's Story

Charlie lives with her mother, Marcie, in a small two-bedroom apartment. When Charlie was very young, Marcie had a hard time finding steady employment due to low wages or an inflexible schedule that would not allow a single mother to take care of her toddler. That meant that Marcie and Charlie had to move several times to find affordable housing. Now that Charlie is in elementary school, Marcie has had the same job for 3 years, as well as the same apartment. At one point, Marcie and Charlie had to use government assistance programs to supplement Marcie's income, but now they only use the state's child care subsidy system to help pay for Charlie's after-school program during the school year and her summer camp.

Charlie has never met her biological father, and Marcie's parents had died before Charlie was born. They have several families in their neighborhood who are close friends, but their family has always been just the two of them. When they lived in smaller apartments when Charlie was little, they had only one bedroom. Charlie slept in the same bedroom as Marcie until they got their first two-bedroom apartment, but any time she is upset or scared, she will sneak back into her mother's room at night to sleep with her.

Marcie tried to work from home when Charlie was an infant. She did people's laundry and ironing. She worked as a seamstress. She also made birthday cakes and decorated cookies. She was able to stay in the apartment with Charlie, but they needed a lot of government assistance, which still didn't seem to provide everything that they needed. When Charlie turned 18 months old, Marcie decided it was time to find a job outside the home, hopefully with health insurance. This meant that Charlie would need to attend child care for the first time.

Marcie didn't know much about looking for a good child care program, but she started by looking at the programs where her friends enrolled their children. She was shocked at how expensive child care was, and she became frustrated quickly when every program she went to told her they had a waiting list. She finally found a program that wasn't too far from her home. It wasn't her first choice, but they would accept her child care subsidy money, so she enrolled Charlie in the full-day toddler program.

Charlie had never been away from her mother, not even for a day, and she definitely had never been left with strangers. Marcie knew that for the first week or two, it would be hard for her and Charlie to become accustomed to this big change. Her friends told her that the first day might not be too bad because Charlie might be distracted by the new toys and faces when she dropped her off. Days 2 and 3 would be the worst because Charlie would know that Marcie was leaving her. In addition, Charlie still wouldn't be acclimated to the classroom. They told her to say goodbye even though Charlie would be crying, because Charlie would cry as long as Marcie stayed in the classroom preparing to leave. The teachers agreed with this and told Marcie that children typically stop crying and begin to explore the classroom by the time the parent gets to their car, even if the parent never gets to see the child calm down before leaving.

Marcie thought about Charlie all day during her first day of work. Her friends had reassured her that when she went to pick up Charlie from child care at the end of the day, Charlie would be happy and playing with others and that Marcie would have worried for no reason. That was not the case. When Marcie arrived at the child care program just after 5 p.m., she found three of the toddlers playing with hats and dress-up clothes while Charlie sat in the teacher's lap crying hysterically. Charlie ran to Marcie as soon as she walked in the door. The teacher attempted to make it seem like the day had been fine, but when Marcie asked more probing questions, she found that Charlie only stopped crying when she fell asleep at naptime.

This pattern continued for several weeks. Charlie cried nonstop each day in child care, and that eventually led to Marcie crying most days at work. The teachers made lots of suggestions such as bringing a favorite stuffed animal or blanket to school with Charlie. They suggested that Marcie make a recording of her voice reading Charlie's favorite book, and they would let her listen to it at naptime. They made a treasure box full of special treats just for Charlie and told her that if she made it through the day without crying, then she could pick out a special treat. Charlie never got to pick out a treat. They switched the treasure box reward to a shorter period of time and told Charlie that if she made it to lunchtime without crying, then she could choose a treat. This still didn't work.

One day, when Marcie came to drop off Charlie, the teacher told her that they were starting to worry that this amount of crying and such a long adjustment period didn't seem normal to them. They thought it might be time for Marcie to ask Charlie's pediatrician for some advice. Charlie didn't have a regular pediatrician, but Marcie made an appointment at the health department and took the day off of work to take her to see the doctor. When Marcie described everything that was happening at child care, the doctor said that it sounded like a very exaggerated case of separation anxiety. He told Marcie that she had a couple of options. First, she could see if a child counselor would want to observe Charlie. He didn't think that was the best option because Charlie was still so young. He said the other option was that he could make a referral for Charlie to be evaluated by a state program called Early Steps. The program was for children up to age 3, and it was a way for children to get help with any possible developmental delays before they were old enough to enter public school preschool.

Marcie was very offended and became upset with the doctor. She yelled at him and said that her daughter was not going to be in special education. Charlie was just having a hard time right now, and he needed to find a way to help them calm her down. The doctor explained that many of the children in Early Steps would never be in special education, even though it was not a character defect for the children who did need those services. The purpose of this program is to help children get a little support at an early age and, it is hoped, reduce the amount of help that they might need in the future. He also told her that the specialist could go to Charlie's school to work with her so that Marcie wouldn't have to take off work to go to more appointments. The best part was that it was a state-funded program, so Marcie wouldn't have any large expenses.

Marcie didn't like the idea, but she also didn't want Charlie to cry all day when they were apart. She asked the doctor to submit the referral. The doctor reminded her that it still would take some time for the referral to be processed and for Early Steps to send a specialist to conduct an assessment to see if Charlie qualified. In the meantime, Charlie wasn't crying all 9 hours that she was in child care, but she was still crying for a large portion of it. The assistant teacher in the classroom changed, and that set Charlie's progress back.

In the evenings, it was hard for Marcie to get anything accomplished at home because Charlie clung to her leg as she walked around the apartment. At night, Charlie wrapped herself around her mother's arm when they were lying in bed and she would not let go. If a neighborhood friend came over to visit Marcie, Charlie would begin to cry and hold her mother tightly. She thought Marcie was trying to leave her again. It was overwhelming for Marcie to see her smart, talkative, creative child completely shut down as soon as someone entered the room.

Eventually, Early Steps was able to come to the child care program and perform Charlie's assessment. The case worker told Marcie that Charlie showed a delay in social and emotional skills. They suggested that a developmental interventionist come to her child care program for 1 hour each week to help her learn how to interact with the staff and the other children. They also suggested that a speech pathologist come twice a month for 1 hour each time to help Charlie learn to tell others that she is upset without yelling or crying. Marcie signed off on the parent agreement, and she partnered with the child care program director to set up a time for the specialists to come and see Charlie. Marcie felt a lot better when she found out that other students in the child care program received visits from Early Steps. She was also happy to hear that the Early Steps team would work with the teachers to help them understand how to support Charlie.

As Charlie approached her third birthday, the Early Steps team told her mother that to continue receiving her weekly support services, Charlie would need to attend public school preschool beginning on her third birthday. The preschool classroom and the services would still be free, but the preschool class would only last from 8 to 11 a.m. Marcie initially said no because she had to work until 4:30 p.m. every day and couldn't leave work to pick Charlie up from school. The Early Steps team members met with her to talk about how other families handled this obstacle. Many of them found a child care program that would pick the children up at the school and bring them back to the child care program for the rest of the workday. When Marcie asked the director of Charlie's child care program about this option, she told Marcie that the center picked up two other children at that elementary school each day at 11 a.m. and they could add Charlie to the pick-up list. Charlie's day would be disrupted from the midday transition, but Marcie would not need to find a whole new child care program.

Marcie could finally see that Charlie was making progress. Eventually, drop-offs at the new school were not so bad, and when Marcie picked Charlie up at the end of the day, she was playing with other children in the classroom. Marcie started to feel that Charlie might not need the public school preschool class anymore and that she and Charlie could go back to a "normal life." Then, Charlie's teacher at preschool asked Marcie if they could set up a parent–teacher conference. Marcie wasn't sure if this was a standard meeting, but she agreed to come in and talk to the teacher. The teacher began telling Marcie about who Charlie's friends were, what her favorite parts of the classroom were, and how much time Charlie spent in the art area. Marcie thought that all of this showed how much progress that Charlie had made in the past year and a half.

Then, the teacher asked Marcie to look at some of Charlie's artwork. Each page had a picture drawn in crayon and then adult handwriting at the bottom describing what was happening in the picture. The pictures all showed two people, one larger than the other, to indicate Marcie and Charlie. Each picture looked unique, but the dictation that the adult had written at the bottom all seemed similar. There were statements about how Charlie didn't want her or her mother to get sick. There was a story about how Charlie was going to protect her mom from a storm so that no one got hurt. There was a picture that said Charlie and her mother were hiding in the closet to stay safe from a monster. All of the pictures showed that Charlie was afraid of something or someone hurting the two of them.

The teacher told Marcie that it isn't unusual for a child to draw a picture of a monster under the bed on occasion, but she was worried because every picture that Charlie drew indicated that she was scared. She also said that she and her assistant teachers have had conversations with Charlie that worried them. One time, Charlie was worried that the man she saw on the news shooting people in the mall might find Charlie and her mom. Another time, Charlie was telling the teacher that she was worried about their apartment catching on fire so she wanted to put a bucket in the bathroom to fill up with water from the tub and save their home. All of these fears showed a level of anxiety that was persistent and too overwhelming for a typical 3-year-old child.

The teacher wanted Marcie's permission to have Charlie evaluated by the school district's child psychologist and see what she thought was the root problem of all these fears. Again, Marcie initially wanted to decline the evaluation, but she worried about her sweet little girl taking the weight of the world on her shoulders with these fears. She signed the release paperwork, and the teacher told her that there would be another team meeting like the one that they had had before Charlie started preschool.

After the parent–teacher conference, Marcie began watching Charlie very closely. She realized that Charlie was watching the adult news whenever Marcie had the television on in the room. Marcie realized that she needed to make some changes for Charlie's sake. She would not watch the news in front of her anymore, and they were not going to watch any movies that seemed even remotely scary for a child. Of course, Marcie couldn't control what Charlie heard outside of the house, but she could control the media and their conversations. Marcie also talked to Charlie's classroom teachers at the child care program. She told them about the pictures at school and asked if they had seen that in child care. They told her that they had not asked her about her pictures, but they told Marcie they would begin to have more conversations about Charlie's artwork and to see how she was feeling each day.

When the psychologist and the rest of the special education team met with Marcie, the psychologist said that her evaluation led her to believe that Charlie had a condition known as generalized anxiety disorder. This condition is far beyond normal childhood fears. Very young children with this disorder worry about typical things like being separated from a parent and the monster under the bed, but they also worry about world war, the pandemic, and other large-scale crises. The psychologist also said that this diagnosis is only given when the child has anxiety that has persisted for a long time and takes up a large portion of the child's time. This seemed to make sense with everything that Charlie had been through, but Marcie had no idea how to help her daughter deal with such a large problem.

The psychologist said that the school guidance counselor could begin to meet with Charlie regularly as a part of her individualized education program (IEP) to help her begin to identify when she is scared about something and if it is reasonable to be upset about that problem. Charlie was ready to stop having speech therapy, which was in her IEP, but the school had a special education teacher who worked specifically on social-emotional behaviors that they could include in the IEP. The psychologist did say that Marcie should take her evaluation back to the pediatrician to see if there was anything that needed to be recommended from a medical perspective. Marcie knew that meant another day she had to ask to take off from work, but she also wanted her daughter to have the best care. Marcie took Charlie and her evaluation back to the health department, and the pediatrician recommended utilizing the school's services only at that time. Charlie was almost 4, and the doctor wanted to reevaluate at her fifth birthday to see how she had progressed with therapy.

It took several months for Charlie to become comfortable with the school guidance counselor, but once she did, Marcie began seeing progress. Charlie would use words like "scared" or "afraid." It wasn't that Charlie had not known these words before, because she had a huge vocabulary, but she had never used them in reference to herself. Charlie was also spending more time talking to the other students at school, according to her teachers at the public school preschool and at child care. Still, when they were at home together, Charlie was Marcie's shadow. She followed her from room to room. She wasn't clinging to her leg anymore, but it seemed as though she always needed to have Marcie in her line of sight. In bed, Charlie still held on to Marcie's arm with a vise-like grip.

On Charlie's fifth birthday, Marcie took her back to the health department, and they were able to see the same doctor they had seen the previous year. Marcie also brought the report from Charlie's annual IEP meeting, including the report from the school guidance counselor. Everyone thought that Charlie had made progress but they were still concerned about the amount of time that Charlie spent worrying. The doctor said that he agreed with this report. He believed that Charlie needed a mild antianxiety medication to help her stop the consistent stream of worry all day long. He also told Marcie that he did not believe that he was the person to prescribe and monitor this type of medication. A child psychiatrist would be best qualified to make the decision on what medication to use and how much to prescribe for a small child. He told Marcie that he knew that she would have to take another day off work to take Charlie to the specialist, but he said the good news was that he knew a child psychiatrist who usually took a few pro-bono cases each year. He thought that he could make a call and get Charlie the appointment she needed with no extra expense to Marcie.

Marcie was able to get Charlie in to see the child psychiatrist in 2 months, and she was not charged for the appointment. After reviewing all of Charlie's past evaluations and talking with her in the appointment, the child psychiatrist thought that Charlie should take a mild antianxiety medicine twice a day. She was able to prescribe an inexpensive medication that cost just $3.25 a month with Marcie's minimal health insurance. Marcie needed to bring Charlie to the doctor again in 3 and 6 months to make sure that the medication and dosage were working. After that, they should be able to move to appointments every 6 months unless something unusual arose. The psychiatrist also gave Marcie a list of tips and suggestions for home and school on how to help reduce Charlie's anxiety (or at least to avoid increasing it).

Charlie is now beginning the third grade. She still sees the guidance counselor twice a month as a part of her IEP, but that is the only additional classroom support she needs to be successful at school. She has been taking her antianxiety medication for more than 2 years without any difficulty. At one point, her insurance company wanted to stop covering that particular medication, but the psychiatrist was able to write them a letter explaining that a change could have a very negative impact on her mental health. The insurance company grandfathered her in to continue on that medication even though new patients would not be able to start taking it.

Charlie still sees the child psychiatrist every 6 months, but when she has significant growth spurts, she has to go in sooner. The medication is based on weight, so growing can make it less effective. On most days, Charlie is able to manage her anxiety. There are still issues when she has a big "first." Before her first school choir performance, the choir director took her to the stage and let her stand on the risers to see what it would be like and how close the audience would be. Those types of practices can help to reduce a lot of her anxiety. She struggles a little at the beginning of the school year before she meets her new teacher, but again, the school allows her to come to the building before the end of summer vacation to meet her teacher and see the classroom. Outside of "firsts," Charlie is successful with her regular routine. Marcie has noticed improvements at home, the biggest being that Charlie feels safe enough to be in her room to play on her own, and she even sleeps in her own bed at night. Although Charlie will have her anxiety disorder throughout her life, it is not currently the dominant force in her life. This is due to a supportive mother, flexible teachers, and doctors who listened to the patient. Charlie has made huge progress, and with hard work she will continue that progress for a long time.

References

American Psychiatric Association (APA). (2013). *Diagnostic and statistical manual of mental disorders* (5th ed.). https://doi.org/10.1176/appi.books.9780890425596

American Speech-Language-Hearing Association (ASHA). (2022). *Selective mutism.* https://www.asha.org/public/speech/disorders/selective-mutism/

Bilmes, J., & Welker, T. (2006). *Common psychological disorders in young children.* Red Leaf Press.

Boston Children's Hospital. (2022a). *Generalized anxiety disorder.* https://www.childrenshospital.org/conditions-and-treatments/conditions/g/generalized-anxiety-disorder-gad

Boston Children's Hospital. (2022b). *Phobias.* https://www.childrenshospital.org/conditions-and-treatments/conditions/p/phobias/symptoms-and-causes

Buron, K. D., & Curtis, M. (2021). *The Incredible 5-Point Scale: Assisting students in understanding social interactions and controlling their emotional responses* (2nd ed.). AAPC Publishing.

Center for Child Trauma Assessment, Services and Interventions. (2022). *What is child trauma?* https://cctasi.northwestern.edu/child-trauma/#:~:text=%E2%80%9CChild%20trauma%E2%80%9D%20refers%20to%20a,person%20being%20hurt%20or%20injured

Centers for Disease Control and Prevention. (2022a). *Adverse childhood experiences (ACEs).* https://www.cdc.gov/violenceprevention/aces/index.html

Centers for Disease Control and Prevention. (2022b). *Anxiety and depression in children.* https://www.cdc.gov/childrensmentalhealth/depression.html

Cleveland Clinic. (2022). *Is your child just shy—or is it selective mutism?* https://health.clevelandclinic.org/what-is-selective-mutism/

Harvard Health Publishing. (2018). *Chronic pain and childhood trauma.* https://www.health.harvard.edu/blog/chronic-pain-and-childhood-trauma-2018033012768#:~:text=According%20to%20Harvard's%20Center%20on%20the%20Developing%20Child%2C,hand%20Find%20stability%20with%20a%20charitable%20gift%20annuity

Healthychildren.org. (2022). *How to ease your child's separation anxiety.* https://www.healthychildren.org/English/ages-stages/toddler/Pages/Soothing-Your-Childs-Separation-Anxiety.aspx

Kuypers, L. M. (2011). *The Zones of Regulation: A curriculum designed to foster self-regulation and emotional control.* Social Thinking.

Lewinsohn, P. M., Holm-Denoma, J. M., Small, J. W., Seeley, J. R., & Joiner, T. E. (2008). Separation anxiety disorder in childhood as a risk factor for future mental illness. *Journal of the American Academy of Child and Adolescent Psychiatry, 47*(5), 548–555. https://www.ncbi.nlm.nih.gov/pmc/articles/PMC2732357/

Lord, C., Rutter, M., DiLavore, P. C., Risi, S., Gotham, K., & Bishop, S. (2012). *Autism Diagnostic Observation Schedule, Second Edition (ADOS-2).* Western Psychological Services.

Mayo Clinic. (2022a). *Obsessive-compulsive disorder (OCD).* https://www.mayoclinic.org/diseases-conditions/obsessive-compulsive-disorder/symptoms-causes/syc-20354432

Mayo Clinic. (2022b). *Separation anxiety disorder.* https://www.mayoclinic.org/diseases-conditions/separation-anxiety-disorder/symptoms-causes/syc-20377455

Mayo Clinic. (2022c). *Social anxiety disorder (social phobia).* https://www.mayoclinic.org/diseases-conditions/social-anxiety-disorder/symptoms-causes/syc-20353561

National Alliance for Mental Illness. (2018). *The comorbidity of anxiety and depression.* https://nami.org/Blogs/NAMI-Blog/January-2018/The-Comorbidity-of-Anxiety-and-Depression

National Alliance for Mental Illness. (2022a). *Anxiety disorders.* https://nami.org/About-Mental-Illness/Mental-Health-Conditions/Anxiety-Disorders

National Alliance for Mental Illness. (2022b). *Kids, teens and young adults.* https://nami.org/Your-Journey/Kids-Teens-and-Young-Adults.

National Association of School Psychologists (NASP). (2022). *Anxiety and anxiety disorders in children: Information for parents.* https://www.nasponline.org/resources-and-publications/resources-and-podcasts/mental-health/mental-health-disorders/anxiety-and-anxiety-disorders-in-children-information-for-parents

National Child Traumatic Stress Network. (2022a). *About child trauma.* https://www.nctsn.org/what-is-child-trauma/about-child-trauma

National Child Traumatic Stress Network. (2022b). *Trauma types.* https://www.nctsn.org/what-is-child-trauma/trauma-types

National Institute of Mental Health. (2022). *Obsessive-compulsive disorder.* https://www.nimh.nih.gov/health/topics/obsessive-compulsive-disorder-ocd

National Social Anxiety Center (NSAC). (2022). *What is social anxiety?* https://nationalsocialanxietycenter.com/social-anxiety/

Nemours Children's Health. (2022a). *Anxiety disorders.* https://kidshealth.org/en/parents/anxiety-disorders.html

Nemours Children's Health. (2022b). *Normal childhood fears.* https://kidshealth.org/en/parents/anxiety.html

Nemours Children's Health. (2022c). *Social anxiety factsheet (for schools).* https://kidshealth.org/en/parents/social-phobia-factsheet.html

Selective Mutism Association. (2022). *What is selective mutism?* https://www.selectivemutism.org/what-is-sm/

Vanover, S. T. (2019). *Does my child have a developmental delay? A step-by-step guide for parents on early intervention.* Rowman & Littlefield.

WebMD. (2022). *Anxiety disorders in children.* https://www.webmd.com/children/guide/anxiety-disorders-in-children

ZERO TO THREE. (2016). *DC:0–5: Diagnostic classification of mental health and developmental disorders of infancy and early childhood.* Author.

Index

ABA, *see* Applied behavior analysis
ABC (Antecedent, behavior, and consequence), 19
Abnormal development, 12–13
Abuse, 68
    see also Adverse childhood experiences
Acceptance, 96
ACEs, *see* Adverse childhood experiences
ADHD, *see* Attention-deficit/hyperactivity disorder
Adverse childhood experiences (ACEs), 67–74
    and anxiety, 72–73
    and development, 5
    and phobias, 63
    physical effects of, 71–72
    prevention of, 73–74
    risk factors for, 69
    and selective mutism, 46
    and separation anxiety disorder, 28
    and social anxiety disorder, 38
    and toxic stress, 69–70, 71
Advocacy, 99–100
Affection, parental, 28
Alcoholism, parental, 28
Anger, as stage of grief, 95
Antecedent, behavior, and consequence (ABC), 19
Anticipation, unnecessary, 116
Anxiety, comorbidities with, 19, 85–92
    see also specific disorders
Applied behavior analysis (ABA), 88–89
Assessments, *see* Classroom assessments
Asthma, 72
Attachment, 11
Attachment disorders, 71
Attention-deficit/hyperactivity disorder (ADHD), 16, 18, 89–91
Autism, 87–89
Autonomy, developing, 11

Bargaining, as stage of grief, 96
Basic needs, meeting, 5
Behavior therapy
    for ADHD, 90
    for autism, 88–89
    for generalized anxiety disorder, 20
    for selective mutism, 47

Belittling language, 118
Bipolar disorder, 91–92
Bladder infections, in children with selective mutism, 45
Blushing, 34, 36
Breathing techniques, 73, 108–109
Bullying, 38

Calm-down jar, 108
Calming strategies, 107–109
CBA, *see* Curriculum-based assessment
CBT, *see* Cognitive-behavioral therapy
Cephalocaudal development, 4
Childhood development, *see* Development
Childhood phobias, *see* Phobia(s)
Chronic sorrow, 94
Classroom assessments, 77–82
    definition of, 78
    noticing differences in, 80–81
    referral after, 77, 81–82
    sharing information with parents, 81
Classroom environment, 105
Classroom interventions, 105–114
Cognitive development, 4, 9–10
Cognitive-behavioral therapy (CBT)
    for mood disorders, 92
    for obsessive-compulsive disorder, 54
    for phobias, 64
    for selective mutism, 46
    for separation anxiety disorder, 29
    for social anxiety disorder, 39
    for trauma-created anxiety, 72
Collaboration with family, lack of, 119–120
Comorbidity
    with anxiety, 19, 85–92
    definition of, 85
    treatment impact of, 85–86, 92
Compulsions, 52–53
    see also Obsessive-compulsive disorder
Confidentiality, 21, 39, 64
Counseling, *see specific types of therapy*
Counselors, evaluation by, 77, 82–83
COVID-19 pandemic, 97, 113
Curriculum-based assessment (CBA), 78–79

Daily living skills, 11
Death, of parent, 27
Denial, 95
Depression
  childhood, 86–87
  as stage of grief, 96
Desensitization, 47, 72
Development
  abnormal, 12–13
  adverse experiences and, 5
  domains of, 4, 9–11
  environmental influences, 5
  genetic influences on, 5
  importance of understanding, 3–4
  key principles of, 4–5
  meeting basic needs and, 5
  sensitive periods for, 4
  simple to complex, 4
  typical, 3–13
  uneven, 9
  whole, teacher's perspective on, 120–122
Developmental areas, 9
Developmental delay, 12–13
Developmental milestones
  for two-year-old, 5–6
  for three-year-old, 6
  for four-year-old, 6–7
  for five-year-old, 7
  for six- to eight-year olds, 7–8
  for nine- to 11-year olds, 8–9
  awareness of, 5
  classroom assessment of, 78–82
  sequence of, 4
  windows for, 4, 5
Diagnostic assessment, 79
Disruptive mood dysregulation disorder, 91–92
Divorce, 27, 68, 71, 74
Dopamine, 63
Dual diagnosis, 92

Early intervention, 12
Elementary school-age children
  developmental milestones for, 7–9
  fears of, 60
Embarrassment
  parental, 97
  and phobias, 63, 64
  and selective mutism, 47
  and social anxiety disorder, 33–34, 36, 37, 38
EMDR, *see* Eye movement desensitization and reprocessing therapy
Emotion management, strategies for, 107–112
Emotional development, 4, 11
Emotional neglect, 69
Empathy, 11
Environment
  and development, 5
  and obsessive-compulsive disorder, 53
  and phobias, 63
  and separation anxiety disorder, 27
  and social anxiety disorder, 37–38
ERP, *see* Exposure and response prevention
Evaluations, *see* Professional evaluations
Excessive reassurance, 116
Exhaustion, parent/caregiver, 98
Expectations, unrealistic, 115–116
Exploration, learning through, 4–5
Exposure, graded, 47
Exposure and response prevention (ERP), 54
Exposure therapy, prolonged, 73
Eye movement desensitization and reprocessing (EMDR) therapy, 72

Family counseling, 20, 64
Fatigue
  depression and, 87
  generalized anxiety disorder and, 17–18
  trauma and, 72
Fears and worries
  allowing child to hide from, 117
  in generalized anxiety disorder, 15–16, 19
  normal, 60–61
  in obsessive-compulsive disorder, 51–53
  of parents, 98
  in phobias, 59–61
  in separation anxiety disorder, 25–27
  in social anxiety disorder, 33–34, 37
Fine motor skills, 10
504 plan, 100
Freezing
  in selective mutism, 43, 44
  in social anxiety disorder, 34
Frequent thoughts, in social anxiety disorder, 37
Friendships
  developing, 11
  social anxiety disorder and, 34
Frustration, teacher or parental, 117

GAD, *see* Generalized anxiety disorder
Gender
  and autism, 88
  and generalized anxiety disorder, 16
  and posttraumatic stress disorder, 70
Generalized anxiety disorder (GAD), 15–24
  ADHD versus, 16, 18
  age and diagnosis of, 16, 18, 19
  case studies of, 16–17, 22–24, 123–129
  causes of, 18–19
  as comorbid disorder, 19
  diagnostic criteria for, 17
  documenting episodes and patterns in, 19
  escalation of, 16
  gender and, 16
  medication side effects versus, 18
  medications for, 20–22
  physical manifestations of, 18

social anxiety disorder versus, 34
symptoms of, 17–18
treatments for, 20–22
triggers in, 19
worries and fears in, 15–16
Genetics
and development, 5
and developmental delays, 13
and obsessive-compulsive disorder, 53
and phobias, 63
and separation anxiety disorder, 27
and social anxiety disorder, 37–38
Good-bye ritual, 29
Graded exposure, 47
Grasping skills, 10
Grief, stages of, 94–97

Handedness, 10
Heart rate, 18, 34, 42, 62, 71–72
Helplessness, trauma and, 67, 68

IEP, *see* Individualized education plan
Imperfect parents, 99
Incarceration, of parent, 27, 28
Incredible Five-Point Scale, 111–112, 120
Independence, developing sense of, 11
Independence (self-help) skills, 4, 11
Individualized education plan (IEP), 83, 89, 100, 126–127
Infants, fears of, 60
Interventions, *see* Classroom interventions
Isolation, 98

Jealousy, 98

Language, belittling, 118
Language development, 4, 10
Learning
play/exploration and, 4–5
virtual, 113–114

Medical advice, offering, 118–119
Medication
for ADHD, 90
for comorbidities, 86
for generalized anxiety disorder, 20–22, 127
for phobias, 64
for selective mutism, 47
for separation anxiety disorder, 29
for social anxiety disorder, 39
Medication side effects
in anxiety treatment, 21, 29, 64
generalized anxiety disorder versus, 18
teacher's observation of, 21, 29
Meditation, 73

Mental health diagnosis
developmental delay versus, 13
parent/family's reaction to, 93–96
professional evaluation for, 77, 82–83
referral for, 13, 81–82
see also specific diagnoses
Mental health stigma, 96–97
Military deployment, of parent, 27
Mood disorders, 91–92
Motor development, 4, 10
Moving, as trigger, 28–29
Multisensory experience, learning as, 4–5
Muscle aches and tension, 17, 18, 26, 36
Mutism, *see* Selective mutism

Neglect, 69
see also Adverse childhood experiences

Obsessions, 51–53
Obsessive-compulsive disorder (OCD), 51–57
behavioral strategies for, 55
case study of, 55–57
causes of, 53
definition of, 51
diagnostic criteria for, 53
symptoms of, 52–53
treatment-resistant, 54–55
treatments for, 54–55
triggers for, 53–54
Occupational therapy, 20
OCD, *see* Obsessive-compulsive disorder
Overbearing parents, 38

Panic/panic attack, 34, 62
Parallel play, 11
Parent(s)
advocacy by, 99–100
overbearing, 38
parenting children with special needs, 97–100
partnering with, 93–103
reaction to child's mental health diagnosis, 93–96
sharing assessment information with, 81
story of, 100–103
Parent education, 20, 47
Parental absences, 27, 28
Parenting style, and separation anxiety disorder, 27–28
Partnering, with parents, 93–103
Peer relationships
social anxiety disorder and, 34
social development and, 11
Perfectionism, in generalized anxiety disorder, 15–16
Personality disorders, separation anxiety disorder versus, 29

Phobia(s)
  causes of, 63
  specificity of, 59
  symptoms of, 62–63
  treatments for, 64–65
  see also Social anxiety disorder
Physical development, 10
Physical symptoms/effects
  of generalized anxiety disorder, 18
  of separation anxiety disorder, 26
  of social anxiety disorder, 34, 36
  of trauma, 71–72
Planning skills, 11
Play
  learning through, 4–5
  parallel, 11
  social development through, 11
Play-based therapy
  for generalized anxiety disorder, 20
  for phobias, 64
  for selective mutism, 46–47
  for separation anxiety disorder, 29
Posttraumatic stress disorder (PTSD), 70–71
Premature birth, 13
Preschool-age children
  developmental milestones for, 6–7
  fears of, 60
Problem solving, 9–10
Professional evaluations, 77, 82–83
  ABC (antecedent, behavior, and consequence) in, 19
  description of, 82
  referral for, 13, 77, 81–82
  results of, 83
Prolonged exposure therapy, 73
Protection, parental, 99
Proximodistal development, 4
Psychiatrists, 21, 77, 82–83
Psychologists, 77, 82–83
PTSD, *see* Posttraumatic stress disorder

Reading, strategies for, 109
Reassurance, excessive, 116
Reciprocal speech, 10
Referral, 13, 77, 81–82
Reframing, 72
Regulation, Zones of, 111, 120
Routines, creating, 106–107

SAD, *see* Separation anxiety disorder
Safe spaces, creating, 110–111
School-age children
  developmental milestones for, 7–9
  fears of, 60
Scientific method, child's ability to use, 10
Screening tool, 78
Selective mutism, 43–49
  age and, 43
  bladder infections in children with, 45
  case study of, 48–49
  causes of, 45–46
  definition of, 43
  diagnosis of, 46
  evaluating child with, 46
  nonverbal communication in, 47
  persistence of, 44
  shyness versus, 45
  social anxiety disorder and, 44
  treatments for, 46–47
Selective serotonin reuptake inhibitors (SSRIs), 29, 39, 54–55
Self-awareness, development of, 11
Self-concept, development of, 11
Self-confidence, development of, 11
Self-help skills, 4
Self-regulation, strategies for, 107–112
Sensitive periods, 4
Sensory processing, generalized anxiety disorder and, 19
Separation anxiety, 25
Separation anxiety disorder (SAD), 25–31
  antecedent, behavior, and consequence in, 19
  case study of, 30–31
  causes of, 27–28
  child's age and, 25–26
  diagnostic criteria for, 27
  as gateway anxiety disorder, 26
  personality disorders versus, 29
  physical manifestations of, 26
  symptoms of, 26–27
  treatments for, 29–30
  triggers for, 28–29
  underdiagnosis of, 26
Sequence, of developmental milestones, 4
Serotonin, 39, 63
  see also Selective serotonin reuptake inhibitors
Shaping, 47
Shortness of breath, 34, 62, 71–72
Shyness, selective mutism versus, 45
Sleep problems
  ADHD and, 91
  depression and, 87
  generalized anxiety disorder and, 16, 17–18
  mood disorders and, 91
  separation anxiety disorder and, 26–27
  toxic stress and, 69
  trauma and, 72
Social anxiety disorder, 33–41
  behaviors in, 36
  case studies of, 34–36, 39–41
  causes of, 37–38
  classroom accommodations for, 112–114
  diagnostic criteria for, 37
  frequent thoughts in, 37
  generalized anxiety disorder versus, 34
  physical manifestations of, 34, 36
  selective mutism with, 44
  symptoms of, 36–37
  treatments for, 39
  triggers for, 38–39

Social development, 4, 11
Social phobia, *see* Social anxiety disorder
Social-relationship model, in autism, 89
Sorrow, chronic, 94
Speak, inability to, *see* Selective mutism
Special needs, parenting child with, 97–100
Speech development, 10
Speech-language pathologist, 46
SSRIs, *see* Selective serotonin reuptake inhibitors
Stigma, mental health, 96–97
Stimulus fading, 47
Stomach pain/stomachache, 18, 26, 34, 36, 50, 62, 72
Strategies
  to avoid, 115–122
  calming, 107–109
  classroom, 105–114
Stress, toxic, 69–70, 71
Stuttering, 45–46
Sweating, 18, 34, 36, 62

Talk therapy, *see* Cognitive-behavioral therapy (CBT)
Teachers
  assessment role of, 77–82
  classroom interventions by, 105–114
  partnering with parents, 93–103
  perspective on whole development, 120–122
  strategies to avoid, 115–122
Teasing, 38
Temperament
  and generalized anxiety disorder, 18
  and separation anxiety disorder, 27
  and shyness versus selective mutism, 45
  and social anxiety disorder, 37–38
Thinking, 9–10
Toddlers
  developmental milestones for, 5–6
  fears of, 60
Tools, assessment, 78–79
Toxic stress, 69–70, 71
Trauma, 67–74
  childhood, leading to anxiety, 72–73
  physical effects of, 71–72
  prevention of, 73–74
  see also Adverse childhood experiences
Traumatic event, definition of, 68
Treatment-resistant OCD, 54–55

Uneven development, 9
Unnecessary anticipation, 116
Unrealistic expectations, 115–116

Virtual learning, 113–114

Weighted vest/blanket, 108
Whole development, of child, 120–122
Windows for development, 4, 5
Worries, *see* Fears and worries

Yoga, 73, 108

Zones of Regulation, 111, 120